Prayers, Punk Rock & Pastry

Chris Stewart

Copyright ©2018 Chris Stewart all rights reserved

No part of this publication may be reproduced, Distributed or transmitted in any form or by any means including photocopying, recording or any other electronic or mechanical methods without the prior written permission of the publisher except in the case of brief quotations embodied in reviews and certain other non-commercial uses permitted by copyright law

ISBN-13: 978-1974476657

ISBN-10: 1974476650

To know more about Chris Stewart and his book visit **http://www.chrisstewartspeaks.com**

Contents

Is something different about this Kid?.. 5

I'm a Punk Rocker, Not a Missionary 8

Gangsters and Greasers.. 12

Chuck Berry and Skinheads.. 14

I Wish I Never Opened this Door 18

    My new Love... 20

HOLLYWOOD 26

    Singing the Methadone Blues 32

Smoking by the Dock of the Bay 37

Ruby... 41

Back to LA... 54

East L.A. at midnight 60

Going to the Chapel 63

Houston we have a Problem 70

    Rising Up from the Ashes.. 77

    Sin City Here We Come 85

    Can't Die but I'm Still Trying 88

An Easter Miracle 95

SOBER LIFE 97

    Stepping it up!.. 101

Deuces are Wild.. 109

    Keep coming back 128

    God Shot Thru the Heart 136

Gratitude or Death 145

So I couldn't tell if it was the pounding of my head or it was the pounding of some asshole at the bathroom door. Before I could figure it out, I wretched so hard the bile-filled water splashed up from the toilet bowl to fill my nostrils with my own filth and made me throw up even harder. The pounding grew louder. I was currently locked in the bathroom of the Wendy's at Sunset and La Brea in Los Angeles, trying to get well. Man, being dope sick is a drag, especially when you're homeless. I remember using quarters to buy candy as a kid, but now I begged them off tourists on Hollywood Boulevard just so I could get high or take a shit in peace in some fast food restaurant, since people were always walking by the bushes I used along Wilcox Avenue and I hated the shame of seeing some human being actually trying to succeed in life while I was trying to end mine. But I'm getting ahead of myself- I just need to get this dope cooked up so I can get the hell out of this bathroom before the manager opens the door and catches me! Such is the life of a dope fiend: one step from jail and one shot from death cheating you of any life besides the pathetic one where you blame everybody else for your own misery and use the mistress heroin to make it all go away. When it works, life is the most beautiful 3 minutes possible, then, BOOM, its back to reality and the hustle of getting more dope before the feelings return. I break the needle off the top, shove the syringe up my nose, and shoot 40 cc of brown liquid in slow and easy so I don't spill a drop. Then the world becomes tolerable again, so I pull up my pissed-in pants, wipe the puke off my face, blow the bile out of my nose and open the bathroom door. "Good morning, gentlemen", I say to the manager and some Midwestern dad who looks like he hasn't shit in weeks, and as gracefully as a homeless junkie want to-be rock star can, I slide out the door into the hot afternoon sun of Hollywood. I have 2 hours to hustle, 20 bucks to get downtown to 6th and Alvarado cop some more heroin and find another bathroom or abandoned building to get well in again or I am screwed!! Just another day living the dream, but let's go back to where it all started for me: on the afternoon of March 15, 1970, in a Milwaukie, Oregon hospital room.

Is something different about this Kid?

My mother and I have different recollections of when we knew that I was different from other kids. When I was almost one year sober I asked my mom: "When do you remember me changing? At what age did I start hanging out with the wrong crowd or when did I get a bad attitude towards life?" She goes: "I remember the exact minute. Christopher!!" I told her to take her time because this information is super-important, because I'm trying to stay sober and don't want to repeat the same mistakes. But my mom continued: "You were about 2 minutes old and the nurse brought you over to me and said: 'Mrs. Stewart, I'm not sure what to tell you about your son, but you have to just see it for yourself. I've never seen anything like it! He has this shining light coming thru him and the biggest smile of any baby I have ever seen! Do you mind if I take him to show to the other nurses?'" My mom recalled that the nurse didn't return for over an hour because everybody wanted to see and hold this shining baby! In fact, my mom said that she didn't actually get to spend any time with me until after we went home because some nurse or doctor was always coming in to see this baby with the smile. Now, they couldn't tell whether my smile was a huge happy smile or a huge sinister smile, but either way, that's the moment my mom said she knew I was different. For me, I remember the moment I knew exactly what I wanted to be and to have in life. I was 5 or 6 years old and playing at my neighbor Donny Phelan's house. Donny had an older brother named Gary, who was a CBA, or Certified Bad Ass! Gary was 15 or 16, had a moustache, smoked cigarettes and kissed girls in public! One day Donny and I were playing alone at his house and he says to me: "Hey, you want to go check out my Brother Gary's room?" I was like, "I don't know man, and I don't want to get into trouble." But I gave in and we went down the hall to Gary's room. I remember that as we opened the door I saw the glow of a red light bulb and posters of naked women and the band KISS. I was blown away and said to Donny: "Man, this is awesome!!" I thought that whatever it took to get a room like that I was going to do! I knew that rock n roll and beautiful women were sure to be my destiny. For the next 30 minutes my head was filled with grand illusions of what my teenage years would be, but then I had to go home for dinner. I also remember feeling that if anyone else knew about my dream,

I was in big trouble. So as I walked through the front door of my house- the door with the sign over the top that said: "In our house we serve the Lord"- and I knew that I was as far away from that room filled with pictures of rock stars and women as I was from the North Pole. Then, I always seemed to go for the extremes, and never the middle of the road.

Right around this time I also remember taking my first drink. I was visiting my grandparents' house. Like nearly everyone over age 50 in the Pacific Northwest, my grandpa was a beer drinker. I love him because he was always cracking jokes and making everyone feel good about themselves- especially me! One day during my visit I went out to the garage and I picked up a can of grandpa's favorite beer, Hamm's. A popular cheap beer that came in a blue and white can with a picture of a forest with a stream running through it- implying that the beer takes fresh like delicious mountain spring water! I remember taking a big swig and thinking: "This will make me funny and nice too, but instead I hated the taste! No fireworks, no second drink- I decided right then that no matter how cool beer looked, it tasted like crap and I was not going to drink anymore! My grandparents lived in a trailer park, just down the street from where my Aunt Kathy lived. She was my mother's sister and a chain smoker and habitual Pepsi drinker who loved listening to rock n' roll. She was also usually with a guy who rode a Harley or had a cool hot rod, so I spent a lot of time at her place drinking Pepsi, watching movies that I wasn't allowed to watch at home, and listening to the music that would fuel my life many years later. I think I developed my love of all things made of sugar at Aunt Kathy's house. My uncle Jim my mother's younger brother was a Vietnam vet, was cool, too, he was more like my hero than just my uncle because of his constant encouragement. He always took me to shoot BB guns and drink Pepsi while he shot regular guns and drank beer. We were like two peas in a pod- even 10 years later I showed up at Christmas with a pint of Jack Daniels and he showed up 30 minutes later with a fifth of Jack Daniels- I was like his "Mini me". One Christmas I drove my '68 Pontiac GTO from Portland to Roseburg- I couldn't wait for him to see it! I knew he would be so proud of me for having such a kick-ass ride, and he was. As I write this Uncle Jim is very sick, but he is still my hero. We've told each other all the stuff we loved about each other that most people never get to say or choose to say to each other, but he knows I love him and I know I was more like a brother to him than a nephew. But let's get back to the story. So, after my first drink of beer that did nothing for me, I really dove into sports. But there was just one problem: if I wasn't the best at whatever I did I would just quit. My 4th grade teacher Ms. Bay even said: "Chris is a unique child. When he's in a good mood everyone wants to follow him and be around him, but when he's in a bad mood it's like everybody wants to go home. I think it would be fair to say that Chris will either become president or he will go to prison." Even in 4th grade I knew that she was probably right, so I decided I that would be president! However, just six years later a series of events would drastically change not only the course of my life but my destiny and my hopes of ever becoming president.

I'm a Punk Rocker, Not a Missionary

When I turned 15, I wasn't a hell-raising kid-I didn't drink or do drugs, I was the star of my church basketball team and was a good soccer player. I also got along with pretty much everyone, but I was a little out there because I was one of only 3 kids in a high school with 1,500 students who had a nose ring, which, back in the XXs, was a big deal! Nonetheless, I was at war with my father. See, about two years earlier my folks decided that becoming missionaries in Europe would be the family plan, and that was not compatible with my destiny: becoming the next Nikki Sixx of Motley Crüe. This was around the time that one of the first very traumatic events happened in my life. Like so many of my stories to come, this one started with a girl, Cherri, who I met 6 months before at church camp. Cheri was my dream girl: she was a punk rock chick living in a world of Christianity. Just like me, she faced the possibility of being forced to be a missionary kid, although she would have gone to Africa or Europe. Maybe if she had been going to Europe too this story would have a different ending, but regardless, after that week at camp we both went back home and committed to each other in a way that only teenage kids can do! About a week after, camp ended. I had my usual daily call from her, but she was crying. I asked: "What's the matter, babe?" She said her parents had just been accepted to go to Africa, she was leaving in two days. I lost it! God knew I was in love with her, but I knew he was already punishing me for the mistakes I had made in life or the sins I had committed by taking her away from me. The thought of losing her tore me apart, because in my mind, I would never find anyone to take her place and after she left I would be alone again. I also knew that I was probably next in line to become a missionary kid and I couldn't deal with that possibility. When my folks took me to see her one last time to say good-bye, all I remember is trying not to cry in front of her and promising to write her letters every day. Now, losing Cherri really affected me because: 1) I was more determined than ever never to become a missionary; and 2) I now felt that god could not be trusted in my life.

When I was still 15 I had a second life-changing experience. I was dating Tana, a 17 year-old who went to my school. Tana was gorgeous, but better still, she had a car and was a blast to hang out with. One day we told our parents we were going to a school dance, but instead we went to the park where all my punk rock friends hung out. We had one of the guys there buy us booze. I had maybe one beer so I could look cool, even though I still thought beer tasted like crap. Tana had a 2 liter bottle of this wine cooler stuff they used to sell. After a few drinks, we were making out and then decided to go back to my house, because my parents were at bible study. Not long after, we got to my house our clothes were off and sex was happening- my first time. I'll never forget it- the best minute and 27 seconds of my life! Afterward, we went back to the park and kept drinking, but I was still sober and she was getting wasted! All of a sudden, Tana starts throwing up and making a scene. See, she forgot to tell me that she was hypoglycemic. The combination of no food and about half a gallon of essentially wine and sugar put her into a state I had no idea how to fix. Everything she ate she would throw up, so we decided to go find her sister at the dance to get her help. The only problem was that she was in no condition to drive and her Volkswagen had a stick shift, which I didn't know how to use. So I drove about 10 miles in 1st and 2nd gear with her puking out of the window- who know why we didn't get caught. We finally got to the school at nearly 11 PM, and by this time the dance was over. I drove back to my house because I had to be home by 11. I parked, left her in the car and promised I'd return in about 15 minutes. I went inside, pretended to go to sleep, and snuck back out my window to check on her. When I opened the car door I knew I was in big trouble. She was almost completely naked because she'd taken off her puke-covered shirt and pants. The car interior was also covered in puke. I remember sitting there thinking: I hope I don't go to jail, because what if people think I did this to her? Finally, at about 1 am a truck pulls up and shines its lights right in her car. Out steps her dad who opens her car door, looks at her, looks at me, and says: "Get the fuck out of this car before I come over there and kill you!" I said what I always would say in those situations: "I didn't do anything". Whatever I said didn't matter because here was his baby girl, naked, covered in puke, so it had to be my fault.

After that episode I did not see Tana much. That bummed me out because I really liked her and I also got to have sex, which most guys my age only thought about. Then one day my father and I had a conversation that would change both of our lives forever. My father said to me: "Son, your mother and I have been more than accommodating with your music choices (I was never allowed to listen to any music that was not approved by them), but we are a missionary family and you need to be a part of that. So we want you to get a regular hair cut (I had a Mohawk at the time) start wearing appropriate clothes and be a part of our story as a family when we go to ask support from other churches (usually when they did that I would cut out and skateboard around the parking lot or listen to music in the car). If you can't do that then maybe you should find your own way."

Here's what I heard: Christians couldn't have cool hair, that my dad cared more about what others thought of my looks than me, and that if I didn't want to be part of the family I should get out. So after a couple of days thinking about what he said, I told him that I didn't want the same things as he did, so I'm moving out. I already had some cash saved. I was a workaholic at an early age and earned money mowing lawns, baby sitting and delivering newspapers. For me to move out was a purely egotistical move on both our parts, but I was only 15 and I had no idea what I was actually signing up for! So the day after Christmas 1985 my dad put me on a bus from McMinnville, Oregon to Portland and that was it. Later that night, I was down in Pioneer Courthouse Square talking with my friend Skindy about what happened and she offered to let me stay at her folks' house for at least that night. After that I ended up at a punk rock house with some older friends who let me crash there for a while on their couch. But I quickly realized that I needed to stay somewhere safer, so I couch surfed at other punk's houses for a while. Until my friend Mel took me in at a legendary punk rock house, Lockjaw House. The house had no hot water and plenty of rats and roaches, but at least it had electricity and I had my own room. As the leader of the East Side Skins, my friend Mel was feared by many and considered to be a violent Nazi (he wasn't), but he was like my big brother and every night when I got home from my job dishwashing that I got less than a month after moving out he would invite me to his room to smoke pot and watch Hawaii 5-0. At that time, I didn't really drink or do drugs, but one day I had a hard time sleeping so I tried some pot. It helped me calm down enough to sleep. About a month after I moved in Mel told me he was moving to LA to start a band and asked if I wanted to with him. I thought: "Hell yeah!"- moving to LA had been what I'd been waiting to do my whole life. Looked like moving in with Mel was the right decision and my life was coming together nicely! I had also met a beautiful blond named Jean and I fell in love. Three months almost to the day I moved out of my parents' house I loaded up the van with Mel and left Portland for LA. Jean was crying hysterically when I left and I did feel bad leaving her, but I still had no idea how painful it was to be separated from someone you loved. Besides, I was just going to go to LA, become a huge rock star and come back to get her. That was the plan, but funny how life doesn't seem to work out you way you plan.

Gangsters and Greasers

So when Mel and I got to LA, man I couldn't have been more stoked. I mean, it was a dream come true. Sunny weather every day, gorgeous blondes on every corner, skateboards that weren't just for fun but a way of life. And Hollywood? I mean who wouldn't want to live there? That place was magic- gold-sparkled streets, the Walk of Fame (where, many years later, I would go stand on Elvis's star before I had a gig for good luck), the guitar center on Sunset, The Whiskey, The Roxy, The Troubadour, The Rainbow Bar and Grill, I mean just walking down the street made you feel like somebody cool. For me I finally felt like I had come home to the place I belonged. But Mel had other ideas, so mostly we hung out in the Valley, Sherman Oaks, or Thousand Oaks and go to these killer punk rock shows on the weekend. But still, compared to Portland, where there was basically one place to see a punk show and it was a 21 and over place so I had to sneak in, LA was AWESOME! There were all these bands playing all-age shows. Fenders Ballroom in Long Beach was a favorite- every week bands like The Adolescents, the Youth Brigade, Angry Samoans, Black Flag, Circle Jerks and lots of other out of town bands would create this gorgeous blend of teenage angst, hate, anti-everything, us-against-the-world type vibe all wrapped up in love and unity for our punk rock family. The pit at Fenders was a sight to behold. In Portland there were only these crappy, violent, elbow-throwing pits of rage, but in Long Beach the pit separated by demographic: the punks, suicidal boys (mostly Latinos that followed the band Suicidal Tendencies),La Mirada punk, Circle One (punks from East L.A.), lads (i.e., L.A. Death Squad- punks from downtown) and skinheads (the working class mostly from the south bay) all cruising around in a circle with their hands up and in the middle would be 20 or so of the toughest, roughest, meanest looking giant skinheads you ever saw who would make sure that the circle stayed a circle and that anyone falling down would be helped back up before they got trampled. Man, I had dreams of one day being in the middle of that circle because NOBODY fucked with those guys. But be careful what you wish- and I wish I'd listened! For about 3 months everything was great in LA: I got a girlfriend whose mom let me sleep over, I got a job at the McDonalds at the Sherman Oaks Galleria- the ultimate place to be in 1986. People like Kenny Rogers would pull up to my drive thru to get their happy meals and I saw a lot of other celebs, too. Now, Mel wasn't having the same experience as I was and about 6 months into the trip he stunned me by saying he was going back to Portland and did I want to go? I was heartbroken- of course I didn't want to go. I wanted to be a rock star and there were no rock stars were coming out of Portland, plus I hated the weather there. About a week later Mel took off and once again I felt abandoned. Being 16 with no money or a real place to stay can really fuck with you. About a week after Mel, left the girl who had let us stay at this house. She was house sitting, informed me that the owners were coming back and we had to get out. The next Saturday we had a huge party and I drank so much vodka and took all these speed pills. I got really sick and I remember being outside throwing up on my Doc Martens when I heard a voice saying: "You ok brother?" I muttered "leave me alone", but when I looked up it was Mike Ness from Social Distortion. I was really pissed because Mike Ness was my hero and the one time it's just me and him I can't stop throwing up!! Story of my life! The following week I went with a couple of skinhead girls I knew to a show in Long Beach and they introduced me to what was to be the next chapter in my life: those skinheads in the middle of the pit!

Chuck Berry and Skinheads

I had met Phil once before with el but I hadn't met Will, Jeff, Sean and the other guys till that night. These guys were part of the most violent skinhead movement to come out of LA: The South Bay Skins. The Skins were a blood-in-blood-out type of gang and were basically partnered with the Aryan Youth and Aryan Brotherhood inside the prisons. This was a time when gangs were everywhere in LA, and if you didn't belong to one you were pretty much dead on the street. The gangs were also divided by neighborhood and ethnicity, so if you were from East LA and Latino, you were a Suicidal Boy (after suicidal tendencies). The LADS controlled the downtown circle. The Circle One gang was from La Mirada, then of course you had the Crips and Bloods and 16th St, which were the real heavy hitters. So when these guys asked if I was interested in becoming a member, I was all in. It's not that I wanted to be a racist- at the time I was listening to Chuck Berry and I loved the blues and had African American friends at work and in my neighborhood, but these guys could offer protection, a place to live, a brotherhood that would keep me safe and it was more like a family compared to the violent Nazi organization portrayed on TV. After all, we had 5 Mexicans in our white gang! I always thought that was funny. Anyway, one day in the park we were drinking some beers and all of a sudden 10 of these guys gave me a 2 minute beating I'll never forget. They split my head open, ripped my clothes, and booted me good, but when it was all over they picked me up hugged me and said what I always wanted to hear you're family now! They took me to a friend's, house cleaned me up and gave me a beer and that's how it all went down. I couldn't have been farther from my dream of being a rock star, but at least I was safe because dreams were a luxury, I couldn't afford now. As a 16 year-old on my own- it was all about survival. Being in a gang didn't change much for me except that now I didn't have to worry about fitting in. I was part of a huge movement and community punk rock! But the violence was really a drag. Every day it was slow cars cruising by pointing guns at you or running from some other gang if we weren't all there. I remember one particular show at the Olympic stadium in downtown LA when the English Dogs, Youth Brigade, China White and some other bands were playing. It was just chaos inside. I remember seeing like 100 punks rush the door because they had no money for tickets. The show started off ok. There were 3 huge pits that night: one was just punks the other was Suicidals ONLY and in the middle was a pit of skins and punks like I had never seen. Imagine over 5oo people in a circle pit just having the time of their lives!! About 40 of us skins stood in the center of that huge pit and I remember the rush of bodies flying everywhere. Everything was cool but I had to take a leak so in between songs, so I tried to make it from the center of the pit to the outside. But punk rock is fast and before I knew it I was thrown into the Suicidal Boys' pit and no joke these guys were in circle pit motion with switchblades in their hands letting everyone, including me, know that we were not welcome!! Luckily, I didn't get shanked but I learned a very important lesson: HOLD IT till after the show was over! Of course, when the headliner English Dogs started their set all hell broke loose. Everyone was wasted and violence was inevitable. I remember being with 2 skinhead chicks I knew. We got separated from everyone else as the cops shut down the show because there was a huge gang war going on outside. When we left the stadium that night, it looked like a war zone: I counted more than 18 ambulances and a dozen police helicopters and cops in riot gear. This was no joke! We made a beeline for my friend's truck and I just remember seeing a line of over 50 cars, including my friend's, with their windows shattered. I felt really bad because her stereo was also stolen and none of us had the money to help her replace the window or stereo. I also remember thinking: "I hope we make it out alive!" So much for a great time. We drove back to Thousand Oaks that night pretty bummed, but also feeling like we'd seen something we knew we would never forget. We also felt like warriors just for making it out alive, especially since the next day, we found out that a couple people died and many arrests were made. The following Sunday I got to go with our leader Bill to Mike Muir's house for a gang summit. Mike was the lead singer of Suicidal Tendencies, which was already banned in L.A. and now the city was talking about banning all of us so we had to come up with a solution! I don't remember much of that day except that they didn't let me in the room with the big dogs. I had to wait in the car. I was already getting into the mindset of seeing what I could get from people- that mindset would really manifest itself later when drugs became an issue. Even though I was in a gang, I still wasn't drinking a lot or using drugs. My life was so chaotic and violent I couldn't afford to get drunk or lose my bearings or else I would surely meet with some bad shit. I'd already seen some really horrible stuff happen to the other homeless or gang kids when they got messed up. Either people would beat them senseless, or if you were a girl it was even worse. So many times I had one of my female friend's head in my lap stroking her hair telling her it was going to be ok even though she had just been beaten or sexually assaulted, Being there to pick up the pieces for these girls was tough, and it still to this day breaks my heart when I see teenage girl who looks homeless walking the street. These experiences taught me a lot about how to treat women. After about a year of this I decided I needed to get out of L.A. When I jumped at an opportunity to get a ride to my grandma's house in Roseburg OR and I brought my friend Lenny back with me so we could recruit new soldiers for the Aryan Youth movement up in Portland. When I got back to Portland, Mel and I hooked back up and after a couple of weeks Jean and I got back together, well, after I beat up the guy she was with at the time. Not my finest moment, but I was still trying to prove myself as a tough guy! Turns out bringing Lenny and this Nazi movement to Portland was the worst idea I ever had. I wasn't planning on it growing- I actually thought it would fizzle out and I would just go back to working on being a rock star. However, the punk scene was starting to attract these crossover metal/punks and the people we had fought with just a year earlier were shaving their heads, getting into the punk scene and creating a whole new wave of violence. About this time Mel and I got into selling drugs- just a little weed and coke- but it was enough money so I could buy my first car: a cherry red 68 GTO. Man that car was sweet!! I remember driving it back from Washington State to Portland not knowing how to drive the car so that every time I touched the gas I would almost burn out. I was never gladder to get home. But Jean taught me how to drive and by the time I was 18 I had a good job at Jake's Famous Crawfish as a busboy. I had a job, fake ID, and a beautiful girlfriend. I was also selling drugs, doing drugs and the party never ended. It was kind of like a punk rock version of that movie Big when Tom Hanks gets his own apartment and every day he and his buddy just do whatever they wanted! Everything was going good and Mel and I had our first band- Tattooed Corpse. We were playing shows, had a 7 inch record at the local record shop, 2nd Ave Records, and I was on my way. But all that just wasn't enough for me, so when the next thing came up I took it. That thing would dictate my life for the next 20 years- HEROIN!

I Wish I Never Opened this Door

Now, I had never been a fan of heroin or the people who used it except for Nikki Sixx and Mike Ness. I knew you could die from that stuff real easy and I didn't want to die- I just wanted to party. But heroin came at me in a very subtle way. I knew a guy named Brad and he had some very rich buddies. Brad also totally normal- he had a couple of grow houses in Portland and since I loved smoking weed I wanted to get in good with this guy. In the beginning, he took me under his wing and taught me about life stuff- like eating Thai food and the importance of having a good suit. So when he asked me one day did I know where to get heroin I was like, no way man that stuff is dangerous! But then he explained how much money could be made with heroin and I changed my mind. At the time I only knew one person who could get heroin and when I called her she said, and I quote: "No fucking way am I getting you into that! Chris, you are not that kind of person!" Then I begged her and told her I needed the money and so she agreed, but only under the promise that I agree that this was a one-time thing. So I went and met up with the guy (who incidentally would become not only my dealer but also my connection to the organized crime syndicate that brought in more heroin than any other group) and then got his number to cut her out of the equation all together- greed was taking over. Now I still wasn't doing any drugs and in my mind I was rationalizing it because I didn't want to do drugs, I just wanted to sell them so I could actually make money!! Dealing weed and coke was cool, but I ended up doing most of the profits so I was eager to make money so I could get back to LA. I was coming up on 20 years old and when I turned 21 I wanted to get back to Hollywood! So, what happened was the next time Brad came over I had scored 7 grams of black tar heroin and when I gave it to him he said: "Do you have any foil?" I said: "Why, you want to smoke some weed?" He laughed and said: "No I'm going to smoke some of this heroin." I went: "What? You can smoke that stuff? I thought you could only shoot it." So I got some foil and that day I smoked heroin for the first time. I'll never forget that day. It was as though all the fear, anxiety and trauma I had dealt with in the last 3 years just disappeared and I was in a state of euphoria I remember thinking: "Why couldn't I have had some of this stuff when I was 6?" I mean, I knew it was heroin, but on that day it became my solution to life's problems and my new best friend. Oh, how things would change after that day.

My new Love

Now, for those of you who have never tried heroin, PLEASE DON'T! For those of us who have there is only one way to describe the experience. Heroin can provide the absolute best feeling a person who is filled with fear, hopelessness, anxiety, frustration, hate, insecurity, pain, abandonment, loss, and low self-esteem can feel. But then, imagine the absolute worst feeling that crushes your mind, body, soul and spirit and then all the feelings you were numb to all come back, but a million times worse- heroin can give that too!! When I took that first hit off the foil I coughed and thought: "Hmmm, this smells like brown sugar and kind of tasted like it too. Since I'm a sugar addict first and foremost I tried another hit and that one washed over me like a tidal wave of warmth and peace of mind- a real euphoria where my current world disappeared and the world I had always wanted became my reality. I felt like I entered a place where nothing bad could happen to me and where it was sunny and I could accomplish anything I wanted to in life. I was no longer Chris Stewart, the insecure little 19 year-old want to be rock star kid, but instead I was Chris Stewart, The LEGEND, and I wanted to keep that feeling for the rest of my life no matter the cost! If you talk to any addict or alcoholic, they will describe the feeling the same way and for those of us who have survived addiction or alcoholism, we will follow that up by the price we paid was never enough to get that feeling back. We as addicts lost jobs, spouses, kids, homes, cars, then our self-worth, self-respect, self-love, self-care and finally our souls. But that final loss comes much later after the divorce, homelessness, selling our bodies and possessions to strangers, doing things we swore we would never do, hurting people we swore we would never hurt and letting people do things to us we swore we would never let happen. But on that first day I remember plugging in my beat-up Hondo bass guitar and when I hit the first note I was transported from a crummy little room in Portland to being front and center stage at Madison Square Garden. It was truly one of the best days in my life, and even though I kept nodding out a lot, every time I would wake up, I felt like I had finally found the thing that would propel me to stardom. How I wished I could have known the truth! The other thing I remember is that this wonder drug heroin allowed me to open up and that my creative juices started flowing like a river so I could express my thoughts in songs and poetry; I could create desserts I wanted to try and everything I thought of seemed to make me more of an artist and musician, almost a philosopher, not just a throw away kid or a king of fools like I had imagined. So, in the beginning I was actually using heroin for what I thought it was intended to do: allow creativity and contact with the souls of humanity- kind of super human. I knew that Nikki Sixx and Mike Ness had written their best songs on heroin. I knew that Johnny Thunders, Dee Dee Ramone and all my other heroes used it for their music, and I wanted to be just like them! I had yet to be exposed to the darkness or the dope sickness of it, and so life was beautiful. Heroin made me appreciate the small things. It even helped with sex- all of a sudden, I could last for the 3 to 5 minutes I heard about from others because I was always a 30 seconds to Mars kind of lover, which was very embarrassing. Problem was, heroin was not a part of my friends' lives so I would have to do it by myself, which I learned much later is part of addiction- the isolation it causes. I always thought it was such a double standard that all these people I knew were snorting huge piles of cocaine and drinking themselves to death, yet if I even mentioned heroin I was like this demon from hell! But instead of listening to my friends or realizing they were just trying to protect me and that cocaine or booze wasn't any better for me either, I wore my heroin addiction as a badge of courage- sign of a true rebel that no one could or would understand. I was a real bad ass and that somehow when I became famous they would all apologize for ever doubting me. That's how strong heroin, or any drug for that matter, can play with the mind of someone who is already sick in some way and that's a big part of what society has yet to realize about addiction. It's not the drugs addicts want, it's the feeling, the sense of comfort and ease drugs give that isn't available anywhere else. So I continued on this path for a while and Mel and I kept rocking our band Tattooed Corpse. I came up with that name one night while I was lying in bed and thinking of how to portray myself- it seemed like the perfect description. I was also a full- time drug dealer at this point. Sure, I was taking a few community college classes, but besides that 4 hours a week I just played and lived the rock n' roll lifestyle. I also was running a grow house, which, being this high profile punk rocker with a fire engine-red GTO with glass pack mufflers, was probably not the best idea and the cops caught on pretty quick. One day I was meeting a friend for a drop off but my dealer didn't show so I showed up empty-handed- another godsend for me because 5 minutes later the cops pulled my friend over and told him that they knew what Chris was doing, so he'd better give them the drugs, but since I hadn't given him anything they let him go. Afterward, he called me and said: "Man, you gotta get out." So I dismantled the house that night and was moved out by morning. I was bummed that I had to give away my crop and let down my partners because they had warned me to keep a low profile. But of course I didn't listen to them or anyone at that time because I was gonna be famous, so don't ruin my high. I got another apartment and opened up shop again, but no matter where I went trouble always followed me. I ended up breaking up with Jean to go after another woman I had met who was more my style (i.e., she had bigger boobs) and understood me better (i.e., she had a job and couldn't go out with me every night). She also came from a different crowd and just a minor point, was the ex-girlfriend of one of my best friends. Then Jean and Mel started dating- and even though I'd just done the same thing I couldn't believe that my best friend and band mate was hooking up with her. I felt so betrayed- he was supposed to be my older brother and look out for me, but instead he cut me deeper than anyone yet had. So the Tattooed Corpses broke up and my heart went with it. I tried to play with some other guys but it was like when the New York Dolls broke up and they started the Heartbreakers with Thunders and Nolan, my new band, was an all-junkie band that just dabbled in music while we followed our true love, heroin. Yet these were my salad days- I was partying, dealing and rocking the fuck out daily without any real consequences. Some bad things did happen, like when five Red Dragons jumped me on the street and ripped off my leather jacket- in the process breaking my collarbone and some ribs, but I healed and got a ton of pain killers. I did miss that jacket though. I'd bought it with my paper route money I earned as a kid and that jacket and I had been thru hell and back, including a cross country trip, lots of spilled blood and even quite a few sexual escapades.

Around this time I decided to really devote myself to dealing smack. I had a great connection through some strippers I knew. I started trading Xanax for dope as well but for me dope, coke, Jack Daniels and Xanax was too much for me most nights and I would get violent and black out. So I decided to just deal dope and get out of the weed and coke business. Although my dream of being rock n'roller was slipping farther away, one day while walking the streets of downtown Portland I saw a stand-up bass in the window of a pawn shop so I walked in. I had always been a fan of stand-up bass and the whole rockabilly scene and I thought this was GOD giving me a sign to get back into music. The rockabilly scene was really coming back in bands like my friend's the Reverend Horton Heat, as well as the Royal Crown Revue, the Paladins, the Jackals, Big Sandy and the Fly Right Boys were all killing it. So I went back home, grabbed 350 bucks from under my mattress, and within two hours had that stand-up bass in my '68 Goat with one end sticking out the window. I was back on top- just 20 years old, but felt like a kid again!

Also around this time I got onto methadone and tried to get off the dope. I took a trip back down to see my friends in LA and while I was there I ended up finding my dream bass guitar, a 1976 Gibson Thunderbird, just like the one Nikki Sixx played, so with my bass guitar and my double bass I was all set to ready to rock n' roll again. But before I went to LA, a biker buddy invited me to go to Ft. Lauderdale for bike week. We would drive all the way from Portland to Florida and see the country. The trip sounded like a great idea, so I said "hell, yeah!" But as much as I consider myself a road dog, relying on selling drugs to strangers across the United States, didn't work out the way I planned and we ended up broke down more than living the high life. By the time we hit Louisiana I was ready to call it quits. In Baton Rouge we hooked up with the Bob Brothers racing crew, a Harley Davidson racing team that was all one percenters- meaning that you didn't fuck with them! They were racing the next day and we were all instructed to go to bed early no drinking!! But I wasn't racing, so I figured what could go wrong? I had a few and then decided to go pass out without eating or anything because I felt guilty. I didn't want to get busted so I took a couple of valium and passed out. The next morning I was walking up some stairs that led from the living room to the kitchen when the pregnant wife of the house's owner was coming down the opposite direction. Somehow I stood up too quick, got dizzy, and fell into her- in the process splitting open her forehead. I then fell myself and cracked my head on the hard tile floor. I have had some concussions in my day but that was the worst plus these guys wanted to kill me!! I felt horrible because I would never do anything to hurt anyone, especially the hostess who was only coming down to wake me for breakfast. She actually saved my life and told her guy and his buddies that it was her fault- that she had tripped into me. Still, I couldn't even stand up and they weren't helping me at all, so while everybody was at Daytona having fun. I was lying in the back of the van with no water or food for over 12 hours, unable to even stand up. When we got to Ft. Lauderdale we were invited to the biggest biker bash of the year. For all these 1%ers, it was an honor and I was only allowed to attend because I was put in charge of the leader, Big Bob, who was in a wheelchair because he lost his leg in a motorcycle wreck years before. I was so stoked- he was awesome and he must really trust me to give me this honor. When we got to the biker bash you had to take a swig of some homemade moonshine as proof of your loyalty. I was fine with that, but then Big Bob said I should go have some fun and just come back and get him before midnight (it was 9 pm at the time). Well, I made it through my smoking weed out of a moonshine-filled watermelon, had a couple of beers but then I got to the upside down margarita station where women with very large breasts pour all the ingredients of a margarita into your mouth while you tilt your head back and then you jump up swallow it and scream, "yee haw!!" I guess after about the 3rd or 4th one I became enamored with my drink pourer and made some comments and a few touchy-feely gestures, which I thought were welcome. However, the woman's guy's name was Bear, and he decided it was time for a bear attack. Luckily he was a slow runner, but after running for about 30 minutes I snuck into the van and laid on the floor hiding under the seats where I promptly passed out and left Big Bob to fend for himself until noon the next day. I made my exit and they told me how disappointed he was in me. The last straw came when I didn't get the money I was promised in a deal and I couldn't get home so I had to get money wired to me so I could make it home for my 21st birthday party!! I made it, just barely, but my girlfriend wasn't that happy to say the least. The two guys that flanked me all night at my party were Big Dave and Big Doug. They're both dead now and I miss them both so much- RIP my brothers. My cake was a magnificent chocolate job with an upright bass on it!! Thanks Tracey!! But I was really stoked because now I was 21 and I could drink legally!! WHOO HOO Let the games begin!

HOLLYWOOD

So I had everything I felt I needed to become famous! I had my red 68 GTO, my Thunderbird bass, an upright bass and a pompadour second to none. I didn't need anyone or anything else- what could possibly go wrong? This time I was sure I would hit it big! I loaded up a U-Haul put that sweet ass ride on a trailer and once again hit the I-5 highway like a bat out of hell, which is what I felt like. I hit LA and through the generousness of friends had a place to stay and got a job working on movie sets doing security. I would take my bass with me and practice at night when everyone had left. I remember when I finally landed an apartment on Whitley Avenue, two blocks off Hollywood Boulevard and I knew things were in my grasp. The first night after I moved in I decided to go to the liquor store and get a 6-pack of Mickeys malt liquor. As I turned the corner on my way to the Pla-boy liquor shop I saw a line of Cholo with pit bulls standing there outside the entrance and I thought: "Where did those guys come from?" Turns out they were the neighborhood watch, as in: watch your ass white boy, this is our neighborhood. I remember looking them in the eye as I walked by thinking that sharks and dogs smell fear a mile away and I was sure they could smell fear on me, but I wasn't going to let anyone take away the pleasure of my first beer in my new apartment. After I got my beer I walked back and this time I said: "What's up?" They totally ignored me, so I knew they weren't gonna kill me and because I went to that liquor store every day, we all eventually became friends. In about a year this friendship would be very valuable when the Rodney King riots hit our neighborhood. But that's getting ahead of the story. So, I had my job, my basses and my car but what I didn't have was confidence, so booze really became my courage. After a beer or 3, I would roll through my neighborhood past the homeless people, gang bangers and tourists to explore. Most of the time I would roll around Hollywood Boulevard trying to find the Walk of Fame stars for my heroes and dream that one day I would be there right next to Elvis, James Dean, Marlon Brando and all the other bad asses on the block. Secretly, though, the beer was not doing it and I started giving the eye to everybody slinking in the shadows, hoping I would hear the magic words "you looking?", 'cause I was and I knew I was in Hollywood, so where was the heroin man? Eventually I called a mutual friend whose eyes I had seen pinned at a dinner I was invited to and I hit pay dirt. He told me that he copped every Friday at 5 in downtown and told him to let him know what I wanted so he could pick it up when he got his. This was on a Sunday and the following Friday could not come fast enough!! Ironically, my neighbor saw my pinned eyes a month or so later and said he could get heroin anytime and had a great connection in east LA, which is where the good stuff comes from! Anyway, the next Friday I'm crawling out of my skin with excitement and anticipation. My phone rang at 5:30 with this news: "I got it, you want to come over?" I was in the car before I hung up the phone. After stopping at Trader Joe's to get some quality beer so I didn't look like a total degenerate, you know like I was a high-class heroin user- it was just as an accent to my nice beer after a long day, right? So I got to his house and he was already face into his foil and offered me some. Within minutes I was back as the king of the world regaling my new friend with my master plan for world domination in rock n' roll. Now I truly had the recipe of all my heroes. The only problem was that I could only get heroin on Fridays and only do it in seclusion because none of my other friends did it. So again, isolation was taking over. Around this same time I met Shaky Dave, a kick-ass guitar player and drummer for a rockabilly band called The Boilermakers. From the minute we met he and I were best pals. So my plan was coming together. I had gotten a new job at Gil Turner's liquor on Sunset, right by The Roxy and the infamous Rainbow Bar and Grill, so every night was filled with rock stars like Lemmy, Gene Simmons, CC Deville from Poison Hell. Even Roger Moore of James Bond fame would come in on Sundays with chicks I thought were his daughters, but were his girlfriends. I remember this one night when Gene Simmons walked in to the liquor shop. Now remember, my first rock star crush was Gene Simmons and KISS when I was 6. KISS is literally responsible for my dream of becoming a famous rock star. Anyway, here is shopping and I am freaking out, like, "Holy shit, Gene Simmons dude!!" He says to me: "Hey kid!", and I'm like, "Yes Gene?" He lifts up his shirt and says "Do you think I'm fat?" and I was like, "No way man, you look great!" He said that the record company was giving him shit because he was plumping up so he asked me which one of the fat free snacks was the best. I told him that the Smart food popcorn was pretty good because it had just come out and since I was trying to stay rail thin I ate it. He brings a bag up to the cash register and I couldn't think of a thing to say! I wanted to tell him how he was my idol and take a picture, but I didn't have a camera or a voice so he bought the bag, said "Thanks kid, I'll see you around" and he left. I was devastated. Here, I'd finally met my idol and I blew it! But it was still a win because now he knew where I worked and where the Smart food popcorn was so I knew he would be back! So I would work Sunday thru Thursday, score my dope Friday, and rehearse on Friday night and Sunday, or any other time we could. Shaky Dave and I got tight enough where we started getting some gigs, but the problem was we would play metal or punk clubs cause the rockabilly scene hadn't yet hit its peak so we would play places like the Coconut Teaser or The Shamrock. At one of our first gigs we played with a band named Mighty Joe Young- they later changed their name to the Stone Temple Pilots. After they played I remember thinking that the lead singer was kind of an asshole. But then we played and this guy comes up and says, "Hey man, I really like your band and the way you slap that bass!" I turned around and it was Scott Weiland, lead singer of Mighty Joe Young aka Stone Temple Pilots! That taught me a valuable lesson about judging people. Years later Scott and I would share the same addiction helplessness his in public view and mine a private hell in back alleys and crack hotels. I always wanted to reach out to him after I got clean, but never got the chance. Besides Layne Staley from Alice in Chains I have never met another more tortured soul than Scott Weiland- may you rest in peace, brother. By this time I was copping dope from my junkie neighbor Bob 2 to 3 times a week and it was like I was becoming this puppet when I had dope I was on but when I didn't I sat in my room waiting to get it. Sure, I still had my job but then I lost that and ended up sleeping on Dave's floor. Losing my job took away my dope connection and my money to live and try as I might, I couldn't get a job to literally save my life, So I made the decision to quit my dream yet again and head back to Portland. I had sold my GTO to get a band van, so at least I didn't need the U-Haul this time. As I left LA I was devastated that my dream had come to an end. I knew there was only one solution to my problem and that solution was 1400 miles north- I couldn't get there fast enough. But before I left LA I took a trip to Europe to see my folks and spend the holidays with them for the first time in years. Now this story really lets you in on just how quick my addiction and alcoholism had already progressed. I had been on pretty good behavior since I got to Europe-I mean I left every afternoon went into this little town in Belgium that they lived in called Lueven and became good friends with the pub owner, but usually after my 3 or 4 shots of J and B scotch and 5 or 6 pints I would make it back in time for dinner and then just drink beer. Man, Belgium has the best beer in the world and I was on holiday! Now one day I went to Brussels to check out the punk rock scene and it also just so happened that they had my 7 inch record up on the wall, so I let them know I was in town and they were like: "Oh my god, we love your band! Come back on Sunday and we will have a party and invite everyone to come meet you." Of course I was all in! So on Sunday around noon I left to go to this little get together, promising to be back by dinner because my parents had some friends coming over for dinner so they could meet me. I remember getting down to the record store at about 1 pm and they were right there were about 50 punks and skins hanging out already. I was like a hero returning from war to them! I signed autographs and posed for pictures all the while drinking some punch they'd made that was going down easy! Around 4 pm, things were winding down and I made my way to the bathroom. On the way I noticed about 10-15 bottles of rum and vodka lined up against the wall and I told them that it looked like they'd had a good party last night too. They told me those bottles were just from today! All of a sudden I realized I was hammered. I thought taking a leak might sober me up, but I hadn't really eaten anything all day. When I came back from the bathroom I grabbed one last cup for the road and that was the last thing I remembered until about 7 pm when I came out of my blackout. I'd had dinner with some neo Nazi skinhead who was a leader of the National Front and I guess he'd invited me dinner at his parents' house, which was decorated with all this Nazi memorabilia. Then I realized what time it was. I apologized to my hosts, who were not pleased, but told the mother, who spoke only broken English, that I had promised my mom I'd be home by 6 and I was late, so she told her son that I had to be a good boy and go! I asked them where the train station was and took off, but the next thing I remember was having this guy wake me up on the train saying man you gotta get off the train now! The cops had already come by and couldn't wake you, so they called ahead and are waiting for you at your stop. I guess they went through my pockets and found my directions on how to get back to my parents' place. The conductor said: "Get off here and cut across that field you will see the main streets and follow them home." That guy literally saved my ass because being arrested would have been a disaster. I bolted thru the field, got to the main road and started walking down the sidewalk when all of a sudden my folks pull up and grab me. They were livid because here I was walking down the middle of the street almost getting hit by cars AND I was over 4 hours late! I missed the whole dinner and made everyone worry. Of course there were no cell phones in those days. Then I remember getting carried up the stairs by my dad because I couldn't walk. They put me to bed and then in the middle of the night. I woke up to take a leak but I mistook my sister's desk for the toilet and peed all over her homework. What a way to end the day. So the next morning you think I would be apologetic, but instead my dad found me in the kitchen drinking a beer. He told me that I would kill my mom with my behavior. I told him that it was just one beer, and I was leaving anyway to go to New Year's in Amsterdam.

New Year's in Amsterdam is magical! I mean whatever you want you can have! So I quickly secured some weed, some hash, and started drinking again. I passed on the hookers because I was never a pay to have sex kind of guy, plus I was looking for something else and then I found it. You guessed it, I scored some pure Persian heroin- the kind they talk about in the movies and William Burroughs novels. I remember the guy who sold it to me saying: "Be careful man, this stuff is strong!" I laughed and said told him I was from Hollywood so I could handle it. I should have listened. I ended up drinking for a couple more hours, waiting for it to get dark and then I found a bathroom and snorted the entire half gram of Persian dope. For a few minutes I was on top of the world, but as I was walking down the stairs into this cool vampire-themed club I totally lost all motor functions. Luckily I landed on a couch right inside the club where I spent the next 8 hours immobile, drifting in and out of consciousness. People would come up and talk to me thinking I was just fucked up, but the music was so loud we couldn't actually understand each other. Why I didn't die then I'll never know. The next morning I finally made it off the couch and went into a coffee shop. I guess I must have looked like hell because the owner screamed at me to get my junkie self out of there- I wasn't wanted. I decided that it was time to get out of Amsterdam, so I got stoned out of my mind, left all the rest of my drugs with a punk rock kid who was thrilled, and I beat it back to Belgium to see my folks and get back to the States. I was done with Europe.

Singing the Methadone Blues

Portland bound, I left in my Ford Econoline van with my records and my clothes and a sense that I was already compromising my dream- a feeling I couldn't shake for many, many years to come. On the way to Portland I stopped to see some of my relatives in northern California and southern Oregon. They all assured me that I could get back on track and that God had a plan, but at the time their words rang hollow. When I arrived in Portland I stayed with an old friend who I used to sell weed. He'd since spent some time in prison and now he was offering me a chance to get back on my feet provided I agree not to bring over in any heroin or dealers so he wouldn't violate his probation. I swore up and down I that wanted to make a clean break and would follow the rules! Yet within 2 weeks I was weighing balls of black tar heroin on his kitchen table. In my room I had ounces of weed and grams of cocaine and heroin pretty much in plain sight. I was back in the game I had thought I could escape. Soon I had a friend named Kelly come stay with me to get her away from her heroin-abusing boyfriend and the lifestyle. About an hour after she arrived she went to use the bathroom. But she didn't come out for more than 15 minutes, and didn't respond even to my pounding on the door and yelling her name. So I broke down the door and found her blue-lipped and OD'ed. Evidently she'd either brought her own heroin or found my stash and was near death. I was not prepared for this nor did I know how to handle her condition, but I remembered something I had heard so I took off all her clothes and threw her in the tub spraying her with ice cold water and slapping her repeatedly. Finally she started to come around. I was so pissed at her because if she had died that night there's a good chance my friend and I would have gone to prison for manslaughter because she got the drugs in our house. I sent her back to my room where she passed out while I continued to smoke and snort my way through the night. Later the next day she apologized and we ended up having sex- that moment of intimacy kind of bonded us. We both decided her staying with me was not a great idea- this house just wasn't a healthy environment for someone trying to change their life, so I dropped her off at her boyfriend's house and we just pretended it never happened. The deeper I got into the drugs the more I had to deal to make money and my roommate finally just told me to get out.

During a visit his parole officer saw the foils with burned heroin, my scale and other contraband and told him either I get out or he goes back to jail. So I went to stay with another friend who lived in a big house. I lived in the basement. I had started playing with my band again and with that came all the rock n' roll craziness- someone always sleeping on the couch and non-stop partying. A typical day consisted of morning wake and bake on some really good weed, then I would call up the man and get some deals done before heading to band practice or to the pool hall to start drinking and dealing coke to friends and others who were starting to get tipsy from their day spent drinking. Then it was an all-night love fest with pills, heroin, cocaine and booze. The life seemed normal to me. After all, wasn't hurting anyone and the band was doing well. I thought this was how all rock stars started out. I didn't really want or need a job, so everything was all perfect. One day I thought it would be a great idea to pierce my own nipple, just like Nikki Sixx. So after drinking a fifth of Jägermeister I took a hoop earring out my ear and tried to stick it through my nipple. Despite the tremendous pain and blood, I kept trying to make the pierce complete. I woke up the next morning with my earring half in my nipple, which was covered in blood, and for the first time realized I might need some help. Not in drinking or drugging, but in getting my nipple pierced! So a week later, I went to a lady piercer, hung-over as hell, and got it done. It still hurt like hell but it looked cool!

Around this time, I and my roommates bought a hearse together. I would cruise around in this blue hearse like some kind of vampire Lestat punk rocker and for a while I thought I was back on top! My girlfriend at the time, Lacey, kind of kept me sane but I knew I was coming unraveled and couldn't hide the extent of my addiction for long. Lacey had a big heart and was gorgeous, but I was a heroin-addicted, alcoholic egomaniac. I know I hurt her many times when I didn't want to and I know my behavior would have sickened even the sickest heart of any woman, but to her credit she tried to keep up for a while. We had a lot of great sex in the hearse (and pretty much everywhere else), but eventually that relationship came to an end. Lacey is still my friend and I want to thank her for never killing me in my sleep. In fact, she probably saved my life after many nights of drinking combined with heroin and pills that if she wouldn't have rolled me over in my sleep I might have gone Bon Scott on everyone, choking on my own puke. Around this time, I started to get my daily use and the stronger drugs had made me dope sick. I'll never forget the first time I woke up and realized I was out. My dealer, who usually slept over because we were partying all night, wasn't there because I had a chick stay over and didn't want her to know I was using heroin. Most people could handle coke or booze, but heroin was often too much. While I was using the bathroom I sneezed and next thing I knew my whole body went cold and I started projectile vomiting. I was in the bathroom at least, but it still sprayed everywhere. At first I was confused, and then realized I was dope sick and the trouble that meant. I spent the next 4 hours cold, shivering, throwing up and shitting my brains out till I finally found my dealer and got "well". I swore to myself that I would never run out again and more important, that I would never let me dealer out of my sight! I spent the next 6 months going deeper and deeper into the disease. I had a partner in crime who loved to party as much as I did. Basically we drank, fucked and got high. Sometimes we would go to see bands or out to dinner, but mostly we woke up only to score, sell and consume drugs. We moved into our own place and for a while things calmed down and I even decided to go to the methadone clinic. God bless Lacey- she even gave me the money and I really wanted to prove to her that I could get clean. But you can't get clean if you still hang out with other drug addicts, which I did because I needed the money. Eventually we both became addicted to heroin and methadone. At this time I started reading the AA big book and the one line that always stood out to me was: "if he was just a heavy drinker, he could stop with sufficient reason like a relationship job." So I kept up thinking she could get me clean or by some random act of God I could get struck sober. But then I'd reach into the Metamucil container where I stashed my drugs and get high. Within no time I had quit the methadone clinic and my day consisted of waiting for a call to wake up, getting picked up by a friend, going to a rented apartment on the other side of town to meet my Mexican mafia connection who sold me what I needed to get well for the day, then coming home and getting my girlfriend well. We'd both then lie around trying to stay high before we ran out. Then we'd drink as much alcohol as possible and hope for the best. We spent almost a year living like this until one day we had a huge fight and she threw a milk crate full of books at me as I was coming up the stairs- the crate split my leg from knee to leg. After that fight, I knew I had to get out! But she left me first- within I week she was gone with some other guy and I never saw her again. I had nowhere to live but I didn't care, so I started couch surfing, dope sick and all.

Eventually I kicked dope and that wasn't easy. If you ever kicked dope you know it is the most painful process to experience. It is a three day deal minimum. I would always prepare with my dope kicking remedy (which never worked by the way) I would get a case of two buck chuck red wine a quarter ounce of high quality weed, a half gram to gram of crystal meth and as many pain pills as I could. Oh and a half gallon of vodka. It starts on day one with the shakes, sweats and body ache but usually I could drink through it or smoke a lot of weed and if I was lucky take a few pain pills to get the edge off. By day two my body aches and fever were like food poisoning times hundred and when you throw in the diarrhea and vomiting you might as well stay in the bathroom then chance having an accident in your bed the weed and booze no longer help so I would go to the crystal meth at this point to shock my body and interrupt the chemical imbalance. By day three the pain is unbearable and I would literally flop around on my bed or floor like a fish out of water unable to control any part of my body and the fluids would pour out of me and at that point no amount of cigarettes booze or anything but the heroin can make you well. You are so vulnerable and heartbroken and usually have soiled your underwear you stink to high heaven and are white knuckling the side of your bed waiting to die but you can't! Then you swear you will never do it again! The next day you start to feel better and tell yourself oh this time I will do it different but heroin addiction is like sex with a gorilla it's not over till the gorilla says it's over. So about a week later I went on a tour with my friend's band, which really set the next chapter of my life in motion. We went from Portland to Arizona to San Francisco and had a ball! At a show in San Francisco I met my next HER, a beautiful blonde hair dresser from San Jose. For me it was love at first sight. We had sex the first night we were together, but that night turned out to be another omen that I'll discuss later. The next night in San Jose she suggested I move in with her and I thought that was a great idea. After I got back to t Portland we talked daily for 3 months. I was working as a dishwasher and staying on my friend's couch. By now I was only smoking weed and drinking, but it was still a lot. My boss Brian was doing the same, so we would get high and drink all night, all the while we got paid! Brian, wherever you are, thank you for getting me through those tough times. Around Christmas 1995 my San Jose girlfriend agreed to come to Portland on her Christmas break. I thought: this is it- I'm free from heroin and I'm with a successful gorgeous woman, Amber. What could go wrong?

Smoking by the Dock of the Bay

To me, Campbell, California is best known as the hometown of Lars Fredrickson from Rancid, but beyond that it's a nowhere town outside of San Jose. When I moved there I was expecting a new way of life that was free from the rain and misery of Portland. I was also looking forward to not being alone and having someone who believed in me and could help get me back on my track to Los Angeles and my rock n' roll destiny. Now, to Amber's credit, her heart was in the right place but she was in her early 20s and was just starting her own path. My selfish ways soon became unwelcomed by her and I realized that neither this relationship nor place was right for me, but we still tried to make it work. For a while we were ok because her roommate was a weed dealer and when he was around I could just kick back and get stoned and cruise into San Jose to record shops and other places just to hang out. I had no interest in getting a job- I really just wanted to find a band and get to rocking, but there weren't really any bands around Campbell except for a band called the Alley Boys and they weren't looking for new members. The other problem is that I LIKED to drink and Amber was a drinker only when we went out, which was only on her one day off a week, so that left me with 6 days of going crazy. Alcoholics and addicts will understand this feeling because of their mental obsession with drugs and alcohol. If we're not ingesting them we're thinking about ingesting them. Drugs and alcohol are the only way for us to get a sense of ease and comfort. No person, job, house or car can give the same feeling! So after about 2 months of living with Amber, I reached a friend in San Francisco and found a couple of cool rockabilly chicks looking for a new roommate. I had no romantic interest in either one but they were def down and had a great network of friends and people loved them, so I knew it was a good bet. With their help I might be able to get back to the dream. When I broke the news to Amber she was not happy, but I think she knew in her heart it wasn't working. I still felt really bad about breaking things off with her because she had done a lot for me and also because I would become just another guy she had stuck her neck out for who left fir brighter pastures, even though they weren't romantic ones. So with my leopard skin creepers and upright bass I hit San Francisco and began an adventure the same way I had so many other times: with a joint and a six pack of mickeys malt liquor. Now, getting back to the weird omen that I had the first night I was with Amber, when I moved in with rockabilly Maria and Holly I went down to the garage that I hadn't seen when I moved in and realized that it was the same garage I had sex with Amber that first night!! Such a weird coincidence, but to me it was a sign that I was in the in right place, even if I took the long way to get there. I was also super excited to be living in the Mission district of San Francisco because I knew there was heroin there. When you're a junkie you can just feel it in your bones when dope is near and I constantly would feel it just walking down the street. Now the problem was that I was white and NOBODY would sell it to me or anything else for that matter. I had a little 16 year-old female friend that I met riding in around in my friend Valez's 50 Ford one night. He and my friends Smiley and Thumper belonged to a car club called The Last Originals, so we used to cruise on weekend nights listening to oldies and drinking. I wanted to get weed I would go to Lizzy's house and she would go score for me, but I couldn't get anything stronger, which I guess was good because it gave me a chance to get back on my feet. Besides, Maria and Holly both loved a good martini so most nights we would share one or two, which would get me thru the night. The Last Originals also had a radio show every Sunday night on an underground radio station called Radio Libre and from 7-8 pm they'd play the oldies and we would get mad love from the kids and rockabilly cats living in the Mission. They offered me the 8-9 pm slot that followed theirs. I gladly took it because I had always wanted my own radio show. I called it cutting the Rug with Hellkat! To be on my show the only thing a band need to have was a stand-up bass. I played mostly psychobilly, rockabilly and swing. Through my show I got a name it was awesome and helped me get a name not only in the neighborhood but also in the scene. Maria really helped me out a lot because he had an amazing record collection. I also scored a job up the hill in Noe Valley where I could get to a nicer part of town and meet people who weren't gang bangers or musicians- i.e., the types I'd mostly hung out with. So all of sudden after years of being flat ass broke and strung out I started to get my life back. I had money in my pocket, my own radio show, a job that I liked at the Holey Bagel and I was starting to make friends all over town. S what would be next?

One night my roommate Maria introduced me to her friend Warner, who, in addition being very pretty, had her own business and liked the same music as I did, which was everything from rockabilly to glam metal. Warner and I hit it off right away and within a few months I gave Maria and Holly notice and moved in with her. As much as I liked living in the Mission I was tired of all the bullshit that went on in the neighborhood. Just to give you an idea, one day I saw this guy walking down the middle of the street just stop pull down his pants and take a big dump in the middle of the street! So I was ready to move into a little nicer neighborhood and it was also closer to work so I didn't have to take the bus.

My relationship with Warner would set a pattern for most of my relationships going forward. She was a beautiful soul but she didn't like to go out very often. Instead, she liked to stay home, watch movies, and cuddle. I didn't mind a night or two of that, I wanted to be a rock star and I couldn't sit still to save my life. If I wasn't having sex or sleeping I didn't want to be at home. I am still like this 20 years later but now at least I know it and don't get into relationships with women who enjoy staying in more than going out.

Around this time two major things happened which would define me for many years. First, I was introduced to a bar down the street from the Holey Bagel called the Rat and Raven. I would go there with my coworkers every single night to drink after work before going home. Second, I started my first food company: HellaKrispie, to make hybrid Rice Krispie treats made with high quality weed that I planned to market to snowboarders and skaters. Too bad that within a month or so of hatching my idea, Rice Krispies started selling single serving Rice Kripie bars or their own, so that ended my first dream of food product stardom.

But back to drinking!! I had a friend at the Holey Bagel, Kim Floyd, who I called Freshie Flo (I have nicknames for everyone) because every night while we were closing the store she would mix up these phenomenal fruity vodka drinks that would spark us up and get us ready to hit the Rat! Then we would shoot pool and usually blow lines of coke for a couple of hours. Now at the Rat I met a group of people that would become my family for many years, even though now I have lost contact with them. They were the bartenders Ms. Vicki and Jules, Jeneane and Lea, and then the drinking crew Creepy Pete, Rickets, Laughy, Ann and Wilfie and many more who would come later. At that time we all loved to drink and blow lines and had a ball doing it. Only problem was that I didn't want to go home afterwards and began coming home to Warner later and later and drunker and drunker. For a while Warner would take me out to get drunk so we could spend time together at a cool bar called the Drunk Tank. That place lived up to its name. I loved it there- I could get hammered for 10 bucks and it helped that the owner Joey was a friend of Warner's, but overall the Tank was still just a great bike messenger bar back when it was cool to be a bike messenger!

About this time God would start a series of events that would radically change my life for the next 6 years. It began when Freshie Flo came to me and told me she had a friend from back home that she wanted me to meet: Ruby. Flo thought Ruby and I would have a lot in common. Now I thought to myself, ok sure. Nothing against Flo, but she was gay, from Maine and loved to rave so I didn't have high hopes about this magical friend because I loved to rock, was from the west coast and was straight, but then 3 days later as Flo and I were closing Holey Bagel for the night that I hear her say: "Ruby!". I didn't even turn around until she said: "Ruby, meet Chris" and when I did turn around, yet again, love at first sight. I felt that my soul mate had finally arrived and there she stood in her Rolling Stones mini tee, red patent leather pants and 4 inch heels with Betty Page bangs- all this with the Ramones playing in the background. I literally felt like Heaven was now my earth and love was my air. We all went to the Rat and for the next 2 hours Ruby and I finished each other's sentences, played all our favorite songs, laughed till our sides ached and yet hardly drank! Only one, well two small problems: I had Warner at home and Ruby was engaged to her high school sweetheart, but other than that for that those two hours life was perfect. For the next couple of months we saw each other every single day. Usually she would come by my work and we would go drink at the Rat until it was time to go home. We never cheated on our other relationships and became best friends, which we remain to this day- a miracle considering all that's happened.

Ruby

I was head over heels for Ruby. We were inseparable. I would make her custom cassette tapes of all my favorite songs and then put them in her Jeep she parked right by my work (being a Jeep the doors didn't lock). She would bring me candy and cool punk rock trinkets, and it was only a matter of time before we started hanging out even on days I didn't work. We went to every concert we could from Rancid to the Paladins, swing bands, rockabilly and punk shows. One night we even danced on the rooftop of an apartment building. After a couple months Ruby left her fiancé and Warner saw us hanging out at a show one night. When I got home Warner told me to pack it up, so I did and went to stay with Flo. Then I moved into my friend Theo's house. Theo was my tattoo artist and would later go on to achieve fame as the owner of Spider Murphy's Tattoo Parlor. But at the time he was just doing tattoos in our family room. Ruby went to live with some friends, Jennifer and Shelly, in North Beach- the cool Italian part of San Francisco. Meanwhile, I bought a 1963 Buick Skylark- black with white leather interior and a white hardtop. Ruby and I would cruise around in the Skylark cranking Social Distortion and the Rolling Stones. I was finally happy and felt like life was finally going to give me a chance, but if that was the case I wouldn't be writing this book and I wouldn't even be halfway through the story. Life decided that things were going so good that maybe a new Heroin connection would make things even better! Just 25 bucks and a piece of foil was all it took for me to fall in love with heroin all over again. I tossed everything to the side and jumped back in full force. At this point I didn't sell everything I had and sit in my room waiting to die like I would 5 years later. Instead, it was gradually once a week, then twice a week, then every day. On a typical day I would get up, get stoned, drive from the Ave's over to Noe Valley where I would call up my buddy to tell him I'm in and that I would meet him after work. Then I would try to make time jump forward till I got off work so I could race over to score, get high and then go about my day. Soon I was meeting the contact myself so every day I would stop on my way to work pick it, up get high and spend my days in a numb fog of delusion and joy until that one day when the contact doesn't answer the phone and withdrawals return. I thought about quitting for about 2 hours then he called and I went and picked it up. I made yet another deal with the devil never to run out so I wouldn't get sick. I had moved to Noe Valley near my work- I was also promoted to manager of the shop. That position gave me access to money and the ability to leave work to cop. Usually I would borrow some money from the register, say I was going to make a delivery (even though we didn't deliver), go cop then come back an hour or so later and get high. I would replace the money from cash sales and by the time I met Ruby that night I would be ok and drinking and doing coke so I was alert enough to be the life of the party! This was a great way to live for a couple of months because I had it all but I was flirting with disaster.

That year Ruby invited me to go to with her to her family's place in Boston for Christmas. I had a valium and muscle relaxer prescription to treat back pain from a botched stage dive at a rancid show. My plan was to wean myself off the dope, get some methadone and just relax for a week, but of course that didn't happen. I really wanted to impress Ruby's family, so I decided to make her dad a really cool old school classic car sign like they had in auto repair garages back in the day. For weeks I sanded, sawed and then had Theo paint this masterpiece and it came out awesome! The problem was that I had used all my pills and had no methadone, so I made a last ditch call to my doctor to get my prescription refilled. At first declined but after I screamed at him and told him he would ruin my life if he didn't refill this prescription that he agreed to write a prescription for half as many pills as the original script. So I was still sort of screwed. So we get Boston, which I'd never visited, and I also knew little of cold and snow. That paired with my choice to wear a white fur jacket and stretch jeans like Kid Rock with a half black and half red pompadour looking like the Joker from Batman- her Ruby's dad must have been heartbroken. He was also probably wondering: "Who is this goofball?" But to his credit he never once made me feel uncomfortable. Over 20 years later I still love that man more than my own dad.

I had scored some heroin before I left but ran out in a day. I planned to go to south Boston and score, but Ruby's parents' place was 45 minutes from there and there was two feet of snow on the ground. To make matters worse, the sign I made for Ruby's dad and had shipped still hadn't arrived, so I was filled with anxiety about that. So I blew thru all my pills in 2 days. I had nothing so I called a friend and promised to pay him $100 if he could overnight me some dope. I caught him in a good mood and the promise of all that cash inspired him to send it. The dope got there before the sign, which had taken a detour at the airport. He sent it to me and that got there before the sign which had taken a detour to the airport. By the grace of rumpleminze and some valiums and a Christmas Eve delivery of the sign, Christmas was success! Now, after Christmas I planned go to new York and stay with one of Ruby's friends in Manhattan- I couldn't wait, not only New Year's in New York City, but I could cop and finally warm up! Scoring dope in New York is different from the West Coast, where most of the dealers are Latino. In New York, there are dope dealers of races, so picking out a dope dealer is tough. But I remember from William Burroughs' book that junkies don't look for the clothes or skin color but instead look for the most vacant eyes. So I started looking for vacant eyes, and after getting funny looks from several guys who I'd asked if they had chiva, one guy finally said: "Yeah, 20 a piece, it's a great stuff- get your money NOW and come with me." Within 2 seconds it was in my hands and he was gone like a ghost. But what he gave me was in envelopes not balloons so I had no place to stash them except in my pocket and if a cop saw us I was dead meat! East coast dope is powder, so no smelling up the room- just a quick snort and heaven awaits. The holidays in New York are magical already, but with china white there is no better place on earth. That New Year's was one of the best in my life- no sickness, no shame, just a couple of days with the woman of my dreams walking through the lower east side and imagining all my heroes walking the same streets: Dee Dee Ramone, handsome Dick Manitoba, Jim Carrol, Iggy, Johnny Thunders- man I was living the rock n' roll dream. I never wanted this feeling to end, but eventually we had to go home and then you know what happened. On my way to cop heroin one more time for the ride home I got ripped off by a kid. I knew I shouldn't trust him, but I was in a hurry because I had gone to the store more times than was humanly possible in 3 days and had nothing left to buy so I got in the car and prepared myself for a long drive to Boston and an even longer plane ride home.

The second trip to meet her family didn't work out so well. We were invited up to their cabin in Maine for about a week. I took off with 12 balloons hidden in my vitamin bottle for an 8-day trip. That was a BIG MISTAKE. I blew thru all 12 balloons in just 2 days and got so sick. Once again I made a deal with God to please get me through this. I ended up missing out on most of the trip and just drinking myself into a stupor the rest of the time. I did have some time at the end when Ruby and I took a canoe trip and did some cuddling on a bearskin rug, but I also knew she was disappointed in me and even though she didn't really confront me about it I know she knew. I lived off a CD I bought Kix Hot Wire and rum and cokes for a couple of days. I was so stoked to be clean after 3 days that swore I wouldn't go back to heroin ever again.

Then I called my boss to find out when I worked next and he said: "You don't work here anymore." I pretended I didn't know why and he let me know that they had made an extra 500 dollars in one week without me in charge of the money and I was lucky that he didn't arrest me since in the past 5 months I'd taken a lot of money. I told Ruby I had been fired and that it wasn't my fault, but once again I was losing it all pretty quickly.

I think everything happens for a reason and when I got back to California I went to the Rat and Raven for a drink. As luck would have it, they were hiring a bartender so I got a job right away. Within one week and I was back to stealing- just a little here and there, but it wasn't so much the stealing but the why I was stealing. Within two weeks after getting back I was in the heroin game again, except now I could go right to the source and have it delivered! Every heroin addict's dream- home delivery 7 days a week! About this time Ruby moved in with me, which was great, but also not so great because now I had to really be careful where and when I was getting high. After Ruby moved in things were going great- I was working at the Rat, we were taking Tae Kwon Do, and one the weekends we'd nurse ourselves out of hangovers by drinking champagne and watching cooking shows on TV. Watching shows like Yan Can Cook and Jaques Pepin was what really got me into cooking. Ruby was a vegetarian who would eat fish, and because I wanted to make her as happy as possible I learned how to make cool fish dishes and would have dinner waiting for her every night that we weren't out drinking or at Tae Kwon Do. My heroin use at the time was manageable and I was really wanting to get a band going, but couldn't find anyone I thought was cool enough. So I just made Ruby my source of inspiration for poems and songs yet to be sung. I was so happy at this point. One of the best days of my life was going to pick up Ruby and the girls from her work to give them all a ride home- I remember looking around at my life- here I was surrounded by 3 gorgeous chicks cruising the San Francisco Embarcadero in my '63 Skylark cranking punk rock and smoking a joint rolled in leopard papers. What could be better?

But I was still an addict and too much is never enough. I could never get enough sex, drugs or alcohol to satisfy the empty feeling inside of me. Another problem that arose was that one of the Rat and Raven owners came in one night and I was so hammered that I didn't recognize him. He also saw me pocket a bunch of money that was supposed to go in the register, so I lost that job a day later. I was really upset about losing that job- not just because I was completely broke and dope sick, but my friend Vicki had staked her own reputation to get me hired and I knew I had let down. That job was also the only way I could afford to sustain my drinking habit. But one week later Vicki said she could get me another job down at another bar she worked at in the financial district. Vicki was and is to this day an angel in my life-Vicki, wherever you are I love you and thank you from the bottom of my heart for all you did for me. The new gig was totally different because I was dealing with corporate executives and stock traders who loved nothing more than to drink martinis and the women with them loved cosmopolitans so I became an expert in the cocktail and wine business. I could drink at this new job because the owner was never there and was also a huge alcoholic and coke head so we were a perfect match! I remember one day he said: "Chris come up to the office so I can show you how to do the books." I was like, awesome this guy really trusts me! I go up to the office and find him going through all these heavy binders of paperwork muttering that he knew it was in there somewhere. Then this huge envelope falls out of the binder and when he opened it there was the biggest pile of coke set up for me. He said: "This is how we do the books" and passed me a rolled up one dollar bill (this should have been a red flag for me), snorted ourselves silly. And cemented our friendship. Of course, I was screwing him and he was screwing me, but we knew that all we really cared about was drinking and getting high, so our relationship would work out just fine. So that was my life: go to work at the bar Monday thru Friday from 11 am till 7 pm, which was a dream because then Ruby and I could still hang out every night and I could get my drink on every day. Sometimes Ruby would come to the bar and I'd make us elaborate dinners because I had the run of the place and I could close the doors and we would live like Gatsby- complete with love making on the bar and anywhere else we felt like it! I also met another woman, Christine, who would become a great friend of mine. She was a hairdresser and we the bar had the "Hairdresser's Club" every Monday when hairdressers working in the area would just get hammered and have fun. They were more into smoking weed, which was cool by me because I got free haircuts and anytime you get to hang out with hot hairdressers and get hammered it's a great day in my book! I was off heroin at this point except for an occasional bit here and there, but at least I didn't have a habit and then it happened: Rock n' Roll! I was walking down the street one day on my way to work and across the street I saw this guy who could be my twin. We both just kind of stopped and looked at each other, but because we were too cool to introduce ourselves we just kept walking, but the seed was planted. I got home and told Ruby about this cool new guy I'd seen and how I wanted him in my new band. She was like, "That's awesome, what's his name?" But I had to tell her that I didn't actually get to meet him, we only looked at each other. She laughed and said I was such an idiot- why I didn't get his name or number? After all, all I would have had to do was walk across the street and introduce myself. That's why Ruby is my soul mate- because her comment wasn't negative, but just pointed out that I never went after my dreams but instead waited for them to magically come true, which was why they never did. I understand now that I lived in fear of everything and the main reason I didn't introduce myself was because if he didn't play an instrument or want to be in my band then the dream would be lost so I would rather run all over town saying that I was getting a band together rather than actually doing it. But not even 2 weeks later Ruby and I were at the Social Distortion and the Ramones show and across the room I saw him and his girlfriend- a gothic beauty who actually was the lead singer of Switchblade Sisters. We didn't introduce ourselves, but our girlfriends moved us magically within 3 feet of each other and finally one of them pushed us into each other because we were literally standing side by side at this point and still not talking! But eventually I told him that my name was Chris and he said he was Matt. I told him I play bass and he said he played the guitar. the world stopped & the perfect harmony of brother hood was born. Ruby and Matt's girlfriend Tina became fast friends as well so we could talk. But first we rocked to our 2 favorite bands and that was one of the best nights of my life. Social Distortion, White Heat tour and the Ramones, such a perfect night!! Afterward, we all hung out over at Tina's flat and when Ruby and I finally left the newest rock n' roll power couples had been born. The next morning at like 10 am I called him, but he didn't wake up till 1 pm- such a rock star! He called me back and invited me to come over. The whole day we just talked about all our favorite bands. I couldn't believe it- he loved all the same stuff: NY Dolls, Social Distortion, Rancid, The Humpers, Hanoi Rocks, Rose Tattoo, The Addicts. This was a match made in heaven and finally life was about to get even better. Within a week we had a drummer and a place to practice, so Ruby gave me a ride over there and I met scammin our new drummer a blond haired kid with an easy going disposition until he hit the drums, then he was a beast. Before we got started I pulled out a pint of Jack Daniels to christen the moment. I took a hit and went to pass it around, but neither one of them drank- they were both sober! I didn't really think about it except wondering who was I going to drink with. But the music was more important and besides, I had plenty of drinking buddies and right now I needed a band. So, we were off and running and we started writing songs and for us it was so natural. Lucky and I just clicked on everything he really is like my brother from another mother still till this day. We started getting shows quickly at places like The Bottom of the Hill, Stinky's Peepshow at the Covered Wagon, Paradise Lounge, playing with guys like our friend Billy from Jetboy's new band Diamond Star Halo, the Lunachicks from NY. We also met other great bands like the Toilet Boys from New York and the Humpers from Long Beach. We didn't miss a show and even when one of us had to work tending bar we'd call the other one so they could hear the band playing. Within a few months we even had a demo ready to go. I managed to keep my heroin use under control for a while. Things were going great- Lucky and I were inseparable and pretty much all we did was practice and hang out when we weren't working. We added another guitar player, Lee Bone, who was a certified New York-bred rock n' roller/dope fiend so we were even as a band: two dope fiends and two straight edge guys, so we kind of kept each other in check. My life at this point was still full of adventure and Lucky, the girls and I would sometimes go to LA and check out bands in Hollywood, while also seeing local bands every week. We wanted to build a name for ourselves in every way.

Now I don't know what it is with addicts that we can never just have everything go right without wanting more all the time. It's as though our gratitude switch is broken and no matter how awesome things are we're just never satisfied. So even though I had the best band in the world and the soul mate I had always dreamed of, I just couldn't or wouldn't quit doing dope. Ruby and I broke up because of the drugs She moved back to North Beach with her friends while I stayed in our flat in Noe Valley. The breakup should have been my wake-up call because a few weeks later I also lost my car- no way to get around town, no woman- I kind of lost my shit.

I started going to cosmetology school at this time thinking that would cure me. At school there were like 800 women and me as the only straight guy. Plus, I got along great with the gay guys I knew who most of the San Francisco salons so I knew I could get a job once I graduated. Starting out I made it to class every day and met some really great chicks who I hung out with. I became really close with a girl named Lindsay-we'd share lunches and do our homework together. But eventually I started skipping school because I couldn't make it through the day without dope. I would usually come home during lunch, get high, and race back. But eventually even that got to be too much, so I just started going in the morning. Lindsay would sometimes come home with me to make sure I would come back and with her I would, but I started feeling gross and ashamed of my habit. Lindsay was so pretty and she really liked me, but like the many awesome women in my life she thought if she loved me enough I would come around. She would just lie on my bed with her big green eyes and say: "Can I stay with you?" I would always say: "You don't want to see me when I get sick, it's not good." That's the thing about being a dope addict- all you want is to be loved but we are so sick from the drugs we don't know how to accept love when its offered. I still miss Lindsay and all she did for me- she was one of a kind. After a couple of months of this she told me she found a guy that she really liked and after that she just quit hanging out with me. I quit going to school and I never heard from her again. Yet I'm never alone for long because within a few weeks another angel popped into my life- someone who would watch me destroy myself every day with drugs but not judge me or let me go too far. The break up with Ruby had been devastating to me and now all I did was drugs. I don't remember even going to band practice or work at this time but I do know I was working in a bar somewhere. But this angel, who shall remain nameless, who came from a stripper background and was broken in a different way than me, would bring me chicken strips from KFC and hold me thru the night to make sure I didn't quit breathing. As sick as I was I loved her in a way I couldn't love anyone else at the time. Maybe it was because she couldn't get to close to me or maybe just the feel of human skin was something I missed so much. It was not a sexual relationship because being strung out is definitely not worth the time or effort to make it happen, but it was intimate in the way two broken toys played together in life. We made each other smile and for that I am grateful. Then one day she got in her truck and moved away to start a new life. I hope it turned out well.

Now about this time I got a call from my friend Isaac and he was in a band called the Cross tops, a trucker/punk band and they needed a bass player- did I want to join? Hell, yes I wanted to join! Maybe this was the chance I needed to get clean. Rock n' roll had saved my soul many a time so why not try it again? They had a tour coming up from San Francisco to Oregon then down to Los Angeles and I couldn't wait to start. The problem was I couldn't get clean before we left, so next is my account of the tour and for any drug addict this will perfectly describe the loneliness and misery of finally being on tour but being so dependent on drugs and alcohol, it is more like a traveling prison- all self-induced. For the first leg of the tour from San Francisco through Oregon we would be gone for a week. In my backpack I packed one bottle of vodka wrapped in a wife beater T-shirt, a ¼ ounce of weed, also wrapped up in a wife beater, 38 ballons of heroin divided between two pairs of socks and an eightball of cocaine rolled up in a pair of boxers- that's it! I wore leather pants so I didn't have to change pants and thought I was so smooth. I didn't bring any bass strings or picks any deodorant or toothpaste- just a backpack of all I needed not to get sick. I'm lucky I even remembered my bass. The first couple of days went pretty smoothly, but I knew the guys were catching on to my addiction. I was like a Sid Vicious mess- playing out of time, off key- I looked cool but I knew they were wishing they had never met me! Getting to Portland was my big goal. I couldn't wait to come back to see my friends as the conquering hero rock star after leaving 10 years earlier. Instead, I spent all of my time getting high and I cut the shit out of my hand with a razor blade opening a balloon and bled all over myself and the van. It was so frustrating not being able to have fun with my band brothers, talking to the fans, hanging out with girls, partying with the other bands. All I would do was cruise around the cities we were playing looking for hiding spots to get high or I'd lie motionless in the van just hoping I wouldn't get sick before we got to the next stop. I think one of my lowest points was on one our days off in August when the weather was beautiful. The guys wanted to go swimming at a lake in southern Oregon. and I remember watching them play like kids in the lake while I would be peeking out the window making sure they weren't coming back to the van while I sat there sweating my ass off trying to get high and just hating myself, my disease and my life. What could have been the best time of my life was the worst and I definitely didn't feel like a rock star. After our last show in Oregon we were going to stay till the next day and drive back, taking our time and enjoying the road, but I was out of dope and knew I had about 10 hours until I would be so sick I wouldn't be able to control my bowels or bodily functions, so I demanded we drive straight back. I made up some stupid excuse and I took the wheel and drove 7 hours straight through the night right to my door. I jumped out, said I'd see them tomorrow for our trip to LA, and called my dealer. He showed up within 15 minutes. I bought another 40 balloons for the following week to hold me through LA and passed out. But at this point I couldn't really sleep more than 4 hours without getting sick, so I ended up doing about eight balloons that day and the next morning I had to call my dealer back get 15 more on credit. He walked out about one minute before the guys from the band showed up to get me to go back to LA. I thought I actually forgot my bass about an hour into the trip and then they reminded me I had left it in the van the day before. I didn't even care about my bass anymore. The second leg of the tour was an equal disaster. I had gotten some clean rigs so it was easier to get high and I had preloaded a few to get me going on the trip down there. Once again, we hit LA and I thought: This is great! The returning hero!" We even got to stay at our friend Adam Stern's house- he was in one of my favorite bands when I was a kid, Youth Brigade, but the minute he saw me I knew he was on to me because he was sober at that time and had a wife and nice home and I was a menace. After my first 15 minute bathroom visit in his home I pretty much asked to hang out in the van. Just as well- I felt like the world's biggest loser. They even locked the door to the house so I couldn't even come in to use the bathroom during the night, but at least I could get high. I ran out of dope within 5 days, but at least I was in LA and I knew where to cop. I was so tired of feeling like shit but, I had nowhere to turn and was afraid to ask for help. After our last show in LA I once again volunteered to drive back that night instead of hanging out in LA. At this point I think they just wanted me out of the van, probably because of reek of booze, BO and heroin, so as I drove nobody talked to me or stayed awake on the trip home. In the code of bands you always have a co-pilot to keep you awake, so I knew what was up. They dropped me off the next morning and I did what I always did, except that I'd spent all my money on drugs in LA and I still owed my guy for the 10 ballons I got on credit before I left. The tour was over so I did what any junkie would do- I went and pawned my bass to get my drug money. I didn't need the bass half as much as I needed dope and plus I could always go get it back right? We had one more show after that- opening up for our friend Eddie's band The Legendary Royal Crown Revue at the Fillmore in San Francisco. It was a one of the best nights of my life! Ruby and her sister Helen came down to support me. I was so excited to show everyone how I had made it and the best part was that I had plenty of money and dope that night so I didn't have to worry about being sick! I do remember Eddie coming in to use our bathroom before his band went on and I knew he was on probation from his band for the same shit I'd pulled. I felt bad for him- he looked like shit all alone and scared when he came out I told him how grateful we were to open for them and how I loved him and his family. I gave him a hug and he looked like he might cry but then his steel glaze came back over his eyes and he bolted out to the stage and gave another great performance-

always a professional. After that I really spiraled down, but before I hit bottom I got a new running buddy. Lucky had moved to LA months before the band broke up. I started dealing, what a great idea right? El Hefe and I were the perfect match- he had money and I had dope and we were both strung out. At first I was more strung out than he was, but he did his best to catch up quickly. He also owned a bar so as luck would have it I had a new job working for him. As much damage that came from that partnership I am grateful that he took me in and saved me from being homeless. I didn't realize just how deep we had gotten until I was actually living on a mattress above the bar in a little room we called the office. That's where the isolation really set in. The pattern was the same every day: he would wake me up, I would call the man- let's just call him Miguel- and he would deliver. Just to give you an idea of our range, we were buying hundreds of dollars of smack a day and still running out. My whole life revolved around doing drugs, eating doughnuts (the highlight of my day) and then going back to the bar to drink my life away. It went like clockwork and for a long time it was manageable. I have no idea what I looked like at the time or what people must have thought about me (and honestly I didn't care), but I also didn't want to let my friend El Hefe down so I never stole from him. I made enough money working every night and dealing to pay for my drugs and at this point I was so connected to the Mexican drug cartel I could have anything I wanted without an argument. Now Ruby and I still saw each other from time to time and I still thought I had the moves to get her back and I always will. We are just like that still to this day almost 20 years later. You know your soul mate and they know you and that's just that. At one point I thought if I could just get her to marry me I would give up dope for good. So I went and bought a ring, took her to our favorite hotel, The Madonna Inn in San Luis Obispo, and in between my bathroom visits to keep up my high I popped the question. She was very honest with me and was like: "No way honey, I can't marry a heroin addict." At first my ego took over and I was upset because I still didn't believe I was that far gone, but I knew in my heart she was right and that I had to get my shit together if I was ever going to marry her. I vowed one day I would but that day wasn't the day, so back to the bathroom I went and got very, very numb. The perfect ending to this debacle was that even after that I thought if I could get tickets to the Stones- favorite band- that she would change her mind. The Stones just happened to be playing in San Jose so with 360 of my total 400 dollars to my name I bought us tickets. I bought us all these drugs and champagne for the night, got a hotel room and we set out. I was completely strung out in a bad way at this point- I even made my own t-shirt for the show because I had no money to buy anything cool. I took a white t-shirt, wrote Rolling Stones in Sharpie pen across the front and on the back I wrote Keith=God! We got San Jose and started the party. We had the TV on with the sound down, rocking out when I noticed the TV had a deal on the Stones so I turned it up and it turns out that the Stones had cancelled that show! I was beside myself!! They said Mick couldn't sing, but I knew that was a lie. I told Ruby- no worries- we'll stay here and party but see I didn't have enough dope and I knew El Hefe was going to run out, so I told her I was going run back to San Francisco to pick up some more money and drugs for the next day. I went back, re-stocked my heroin supply and got some coke for Ruby. We hung out and it was fun, but I always hated the anxiety of being sick around her and felt like such a loser. The next day we hung out, started partying getting ready for the show and then they cancelled again. At this point I was over it. I didn't think anything was ever going to go my way again and this was god just punishing me for all the shit I had done and for being a heroin addict. We got wasted that night and went home thinking we would never see the Stones together…

Back to LA

So finally all things run their course and with Ruby out of my life I was only concerned about two things: heroin and more heroin, but I couldn't do enough of anything to get over losing her, the failure of my band and living on a mattress on the floor of an office above a bar. At 29 I hadn't accomplished anything I'd hoped to. Prayers entered the picture at this point, but they weren't the "Dear God, thank you for this and that and please help me be a better man"-type, but instead were along the lines of the title of one of my favorite books: "Please Kill Me". I would be drunk or at least drinking every waking minute at and would start each day with at least 2 grams of black tar heroin just to get me through the day. Most days I would run out by 6 pm, which wouldn't seem that bad if I wasn't waking up at noon. So I put myself on a maintenance program of only getting high every hour on the hour and then drinking and smoking weed in between, which seemed to work. I only used cocaine after 9 pm so I could drink enough to pass out by 2 am. I never understood the whole staying up for days on coke thing. I never would make it past 4 or 5 am even if I was smoking it and snorting it all night- just the way I'm wired I guess.

Eventually El Hefe let me move into his flat so we could just get high constantly- misery loves company? He was a great friend, but the relationship was just a drug buddy and the days of us discussing anything other than how good or not good our dope was were long gone. So every night we would drink and smoke, snort ourselves into oblivion, blaming the world for our problems and hoping that everything would just work out and that our failed relationships, jobs and outlook on life would return to the way it had been 6 months prior, but it never did.

Now here is also when the power of brotherhood comes into play. Evidently someone had talked to Lucky who had married. He was living in Long Beach with his beautiful new wife but he wasn't happy with himself or his career as a musician. Word got to him I was like the living dead and that soon I would be dead and could he talk to me? So one day I got a call on the bar phone. The day bartender came upstairs and after pounding on the door for 10 minutes finally woke me up, even though it was 3 in the afternoon. I asked her to take a message she said it was someone named Lucky. I jumped out of my sweaty, junky sheets and ran downstairs, picked up the phone and said: "Lucky?!!" He was like: "Fumari, my brother, how are you?" I said: "Oh, you know, man not bad, just you know, trying to put together a band and stuff, which was a total lie and he knew it. The thing about best friends is that they know you're lying and your ego is hanging by a thread, so he said: "Cool, me too." Then he said: "Hey man I talked to my wife and she said you could move in with us down here and we could put the Altar Boys back together. Once again he knew if he made it about him asking me I would say no cause my pride was still hurting from our previous break up but if she wanted us back together as a band how could I say no? He also knew I never could say no to a woman- either then or now! So I accepted his offer and thought that maybe a month or two that would give me time to get on methadone, clean up my habit and make a fresh start. Instead, a week later he drove up in his pickup in the rain for 7 hours- literally threw me my amps and clothes in his truck and we drove back to LA that same day That brother had not only driven over 16 hours total but he never once said I looked like shit (which I know I did) or did he give me any heartache for screwing up my life. He also didn't brag that he was responsible for just saving my life. Instead he just said how much he missed me and how now the best team in Rock n' Roll besides Nikki and Tommy or Steven and Joe was about to conquer the world! I couldn't wait to get to Long Beach though because I couldn't go longer than 6 hours without dope and didn't know how to address that situation. By the time we got there I was getting sick but luckily it was so late when we got there after meeting Mrs. Lucky I went into the room they graciously had set up for me and got well. I had 9 grams of heroin on me so I had to think fast because that wasn't even enough for the week. The next day I surveyed the scene and decided this was god helping me out and decided to get clean by weaning myself off dope, which lasted about 3 days before I called my dealer in SF and asked him to send me something in the mail with payment to be made next week. He sent me some, but it wasn't enough and I ended up getting sick, like real sick, and the gig was up. Lucky and his wife both knew that type of sickness and when I just randomly threw up on the floor of the apartment they said that they'd had enough. They said I could stay with them on the condition I get clean. I said I would and I did with their love and help, and then we got busy putting the band back together! There were a few trips back and forth between LA and SF when I copped some heroin, but for the most part I kept my end of the bargain. Mrs. Lucky even let me work with her at her salon on the weekends as her assistant so I would have cigarette and gas money for the week. She was a sweetheart and I never got to thank her for all she did for us.

We got the band going again and started booking shows up in Hollywood where, as luck would have it, I ran into ruby at one of our shows. She was with some other guy so we just traded new numbers and left it at that. Now here is the magic that is my life with Ruby, God and Rock n' Roll. I got a letter in the mail from Ticketmaster saying that the Stones make-up show was finally scheduled for San Jose, but now Ruby and I were both in LA! A good 8 hour drive and she had a boyfriend, but I still called her and said the Stones are playing in a couple weeks in San Jose- do you want to go? She was like, "Hell Yes!" So a couple weeks later I picked her up and she was wearing some khaki pant things and a white t-shirt and I was like- what in the hell is up with that outfit? See I ALWAYS dressed rock no matter what! She said we're just driving and I said no way in hell I'm going to be seen with you in that outfit! So I pulled over and she changed into her rock clothes and we were off!! We had the best time ever- I was so grateful to be off dope so I could actually have fun and not worry about getting sick! We got up to San Jose, got our room and got ready to rock! Now I was nowhere near being sober- I was just off heroin so I was definitely drinking and smoking, but it was just great being with my best friend going to see one of our favorite bands. There was just one challenge: when they cancelled the first show I had traded my really great tickets for some nose bleed seats for the second night show cause that's all that was left, and for the make-up show those were our seats. Let's just say that I'm a man of opportunity (some would say a hustler) and I'm even better when I'm properly inebriated, so we get to the area, I've got a great buzz, and we're going up to our seats on the third level when I noticed a group of about 10 people going to their first level seats. They were totally wasted, so I told Ruby to follow my lead and came up behind them. I started laughing like I knew them- they looked like a corporate work party- people who didn't really know each other that well so they just kind of accepted us. We get up to the top of the stairs where they check the tickets and it's some old guy so as I go to hand him my ticket I pretend to slip and fall down the stairs screaming. The guy freaks out, asks is I'm OK and I tell him: "No, I'm not OK- I almost fell down and broke my back- you need to get this floor fixed before someone really falls down!" He was so busy asking me if I was ok I grabbed Ruby's hand and said just be more careful to him as I called out to our new friends wait up Next thing you know we were like 20 rows off the floor in someone's corporate box on Ronnie's side the people just kept looking at us but no one had the balls to ask if we belonged there and then the stones came on and you know after that we were all one!! One of the best nights and stories of rock n roll ever. Keith when you read this just know I was still wearing that homemade shirt I had made with Keith=god on the back and everyone in our section LOVED it!! Ha-ha

The band was doing great playing shows and becoming staples of the Hollywood scene but unfortunately my drinking was becoming a problem again so when Lucky and his wife moved into their new place I was not invited which really pissed me off and upset me. I mean don't get me wrong I had lived rent free for over a year with them and it was time to move on but I still didn't have my shit together enough to move so I ended sharing an apt up in Hollywood with a mutual friend of ours but it was a cockroach infested dump in the east part of Hollywood and within a week I was hanging out a block away at a crack house smoking crack every chance I got with a couple of homeless guys I met but I wasn't do heroin so I thought it was ok just malt liquor and crack. But before I left Long beach I had one of what I would later come to know as a god shot! One Saturday after they had moved I was sitting in this completely empty apartment with just a clock radio and a bunch of change they had left on the floor of their bedroom which I would scrounge up to get an airplane bottle of booze when the sickness came on me. However on this particular day I was listening to my favorite radio show called Nothing but the blues with Gary "the Wagman" Wagner and on this particular Saturday the Wagman asked a trivia question about BB Kings 1st guitar player and I called in thinking what's the point right? But on this day the heavens shined down and they answered you're the 7th caller what's the answer and I answered Arthur Adams! Congrats you have just won 2 tickets to see him tonight in Hollywood at BB kings club! Man I was so excited but there was only a couple of challenges A. I had no car B. I had no money! But I am a resourceful man when I what to get my way so I went down to my neighbor Amy's house and asked her if she wanted to go? She was a rad neighbor into punk rock and she worked for Roxy clothing at the time she was like no problem but I have no gas or money so then I went to my other neighbors house a cool Harley riding AA chick and asked her for 20 bucks so Amy and I could go and she was like sure! So Amy and I got all dressed up and went to the show it was a blast and made me realize that regardless of whatever situation you're in there is always a way to get help for your cause you just need to ask for it. Now at this point Ruby and I were hanging again as friends so I really was trying to get my shit together I got a job working on Melrose at a cool vintage clothing store but I was always hung-over or still drunk at work every day so I found a solution go back to taking cash sales as no sales and pocketing the money which I used to but large amounts of coke and a bunch of clothes too cause I was determined to be a Rock star still!! Now that I lived in Hollywood and the rest of the band lived in Long beach we pretty much broke up I think it was apparent that I was just an alcoholic who dabbled in music when the rest of the guys were both in serious relationships and looking for something different. Now about this time my friend from SF came to visit her name was dawn and she is one of my besties still to this day. Anyway she was on the guest list to go see our friends band open for the cult at the House of Blues on Sunset Blvd. and after we saw them play we went backstage and there I met a guy who would become my next best friend for many years Les I asked him one simple question you want to get high and he said fuck yea! Done and done we were inseparable after that and it turns out he played bass too but wanted to sing instead so I became the new bass player in City Girls Boys with him a glam rock /sleezy Hollywood type deal and we took off running we went out every single night to pass out flyers and get as drunk and high as possible what a glorious time. I mean we were always at the Bo or Rainbow bar and grill hanging with Lemmy from Motorhead, B-real from cypress hill, Chris Holmes from wasp and everyone else who was anybody! It was the best time of my life! Our days would consist of me going to work so I could get money and cocaine then pick up Les go to practice then hit the strip until late and do it all over again. I mean our band was awesome don't get me wrong we had Matt on guitar who later saved my ass by getting me a job where he worked and remains a great friend to this day not to mention he is now the guitarist for Puddle of Mudd so glad he is getting paid to do what he loves and when Wes wants to get sober Matt knows he can call me. Then there was the blues man Steve "sex" Soto another brother for life jerry was our drummer and he also stayed in touch and is now on my side of sobriety but at the time we drank and drug up Hollywood with the best of them. Now also at this time Ruby and I had gotten back together and I had gotten that day job with matt at an online toy company called Etoys.com which was a great job while it lasted I met a lot of great people including our CEO Toby Lenk who insisted we call him toby never boss. So you think with my great new job a band and ruby back in life I would straighten up right? Oh I wish that was the case but then I wouldn't be writing this book now would I? Now Ruby and I both worked in Santa Monica at this time it was so cool that we ended up working in the same building but we were still living in Hollywood and so our commute was a nightmare most days and we worked different hours so we couldn't even car pool together but that was ok. We both worked Monday thru Friday and the weekends were for partying and a new tradition I started with her. Every Saturday we would go to the farmers market off Fairfax and but some new kind of food we had never tried or a fish or something then I would go home and get stoned and watch that show the IRON CHEF on food network and I would get inspired and go cook some cool thing sometimes it worked sometimes not but after a couple hours of wine and cocktails and whatever else we could get our hands it didn't really matter what I created. But it was how I learned to cook and we had a blast then it would be off to see a band or hit the strip something fun we were having the best time of our lives.

East L.A. at midnight

After about a year of this we decided to move and we found a super cute little house in Culver City it was pink stucco about 3 miles from the Santa Monica beach it even had a detached garage for me and birds of paradise flowers that flanked the front door, a patio with a built in fire pit BBQ. It was paradise and I could not believe this was my life I had finally achieved everything I wanted besides a platinum record. I took to being a suburban neighborhood guy like Clark Griswold at 1st but eventually the drugs came back in and I spent most of my time drinking and getting high but also getting projects done like re doing the hard wood floors and completely remodeling the kitchen. After a couple months living out here Ruby surprised me by telling me she had booked a room at the Madonna in for us for the weekend. I was a little apprehensive at first because of the last time we had been there and my botched wedding proposal but I was clean now off heroin at least so I said let's go! We got there and of course that place is like magic so when we went to have lunch I thought nothing about the fact that we were in the restaurant by ourselves when all of sudden they wheeled out a huge cake and it said will you marry me? I was speechless!! That awkward pause almost ruined it! But of course I said yes I mean she was and is my best friend still to this day but the pause let me explain that. See as an addict I wasn't sure if I could stay clean for life yet? Also I have the disease of selfishness and even though I was elated and beyond happy to be engaged to her my pride was a little bit hurt that I didn't get to ask her? It might seem stupid to some people but ego is the chief defect of addicts and the fact that she now got credit for our marriage somehow gave me a small resentment which would manifest itself later because at the time I didn't understand that was what was happening. But that could all wait because we were going to pop the champagne line up the rails and get the party started!! We called everyone and as usual I was the last to know everyone else was like yea she has been planning this forever! She even had custom made rings for us Ruby's and crowns they were bad ass!! But the bliss was short lived because that Monday at work my friend and coworker wanted to celebrate with me so we took a trip to east LA just to get some weed but you know me and once I felt the heroin radar go up as we were getting the weed I blurted out hey man you got any chiva? His name was Rambo and he fit the name and he became my life line to the Mexican heroin connection running thru LA it was a trip dealing with him because he didn't speak any English and I didn't really speak any Spanish but every morning at 10 am we would meet six days a week to do business. Sometimes I would show up to a hot dog truck and buy a 50 bag of Cheetos containing what I needed other times it would come in a new pair of shoes that I would have to tear the soles off to get the stuff and other times he would just spit eight ballons in to my hand in the middle of the street. The thing about being a heroin addict is that once you get that 1st hit in you everything else disappears and sometime between the engagement and the marriage I was back to being completely strung out. Now Ruby didn't notice at 1st or at least pretended not to notice I had also picked up a new trick where in order to pass the visual test of having my eyes be pinned I had started doing crystal or Tina as we called it. I had a friend named Davis who I had met years before and he was always holding so I was able to do the crystal to make my eyes right sized again I also would quit doing dope by 6 so when she got home at 8 or 9 I would seem fine. However the powers that be were not in my favor plus I was going to AA at the same time too so I'm sure the powers of good and evil were alive and kicking ripping my soul to shreds and surely causing my addiction and selfishness to destroy not only my marriage but any hope I had of ever getting off the dope. Now 30 years old I also lost my job at Etoys like so many dot coms at the time we ran out of funding and we went out of business so 500 others and me were out on our ass. I tried looking for work but being addicted to heroin is a full time job in itself so I wasn't having any luck finding anything. At this point I really wanted to call off the wedding but I still thought I could get clean in time which was a laugh. My days turned into a ridiculous ground hog day like in that movie permanent midnight with ben stiller. I would get up when Ruby was in the shower run to 7-11 withdraw money with her debit card run back to the house and jump back in bed before she was out of the shower. Then the minute she left the house I would call Rambo and head to east LA where I would meet him then because I would be dope sick by then I would drive around till I found a spot to get high usually in the home depot parking lot in between work trucks or in some neighborhood in west LA that was run down sometimes I would go to abandoned buildings in downtown if I was down there meeting him. Then I would drive around and try and figure my next move usually stopping by other junkies houses or other drug dealers houses where we would sit and get high while listening to music or talking about our next great band or ADVENTURE which would never materialize. Around 3 I would head into Hollywood to get my crystal and hang out with davis till 6 or so then drive back home make dinner and start my nightly drinking usually a bottle or 2 of wine or a bottle of vodka or 12 pack of beer or all of it combined then Ruby would get home and we would watch TV till 11 or so go to bed and start it all over the next day. I hated living my double life it's like at night I was this suburban house husband and during the day I was the want to be gangster going into predominately Mexican gang run neighborhoods (like in that movie training day) how I was never actually shot or I never overdosed is beyond me. I thought I was a bad ass copping in Thompkins square park just like my heroes Johnny thunders and Dee Dee Ramone used to do but looking back I am so lucky god had his eye on me. I could easily have ended up in jail or dead because the game in NYC is way more hardcore than the game in LA if you don't know anyone to cop from I mean NYC is a wasteland when it comes to heroin and crack houses. One of the times that made me really feel like shit about myself was copping from this 11 or 12 year old kid up on 10th and A but you know his stuff was way better than the other guys on the street so I always went back to him when I could justifying it by thinking he was actually getting the money for his family.

Going to the Chapel

So at this time it was around July or Aug of 2000 and I knew I had to get sober or I was going to lose everything that I had. The wedding was coming up at the end of October and I was determined to be completely clean AND sober by then. Which was a huge feat and one looking back on would have been impossible for me to do the way I was living. My 1st experience with AA was a phone call to central office in west LA and went like this thanks for calling the AA hotline this is Chris how can I help you? I went oh this is awesome my name is Chris too! Then he asked are you an alcoholic to which I replied yea and I can't stop drinking man it's so frustrating! Then he said well why don't you tell me a little bit about your story so I did leaving out all of the heroin and other drugs because in my head I thought if I was completely honest they wouldn't help me in my mind they would be we can't help you. So I just stuck to the drinking he then suggested that I go to an AA meeting and I got along so well with him I said sure! We were laughing and becoming friends so quickly I thought how hard can this be? This guy gets me! I asked if he would be there and he said he couldn't make that one but he would see me at another one. So on this Monday night I set out to this meeting it was 2 miles away and I was so afraid they would take away my keys after I told them how much I drank that I buried them in the back yard under a flower bush. So I started walking but the road split off into 2 streets halfway there and I took the wrong street down culver Blvd. not culver way so I ended up getting there almost 45 minutes late I was beside myself that I had screwed up so bad! But the worst part was getting home that night because ruby had went and bought me 2 six packs of my favorite Hansen's sodas black cherry and mandarin lime to support me in the not drinking and I had to tell her that I screwed up and took the wrong street and missed the meeting I was so broken I remember just laying on our bed and crying because I thought I was hopeless. The next day however I took my car and went to the meeting and I'll never forget sitting there relieved to finally be in a meeting until this guy got up to share and he said and I quote "the hardest thing I ever had to do was a 4th and 5th step and I remember looking at this Ned Flanders looking guy with his green v neck sweater and khaki pants brown hair parted in the middle and horn rimmed glasses and going FUCK if it was that hard for that guy how is a rock n roll junkie dirt bag like myself ever gonna be able to do it? I felt even more hopeless and decided right then and there that I would get sober but not do those steps no way! So I tried that and it worked for a little while or I should say I was able to quit drinking for a while but no matter what I did I could not get off the heroin the withdrawals were just too painful plus ruby knew by now what the dope sickness looked like and I did not want to screw up any worse but letting her know I was strung out. So now my days consisted of getting up copping from Rambo then going to the noon meeting in Culver City then going home and getting well. Now about this time ruby went out of town for work so I decided this was my chance to kick and I did. Now the only way I describe being dope sick is that it is the absolute worst feeling that I have ever felt. It is almost like what I imagine an exorcism must be like. The 1st day it feels like the flu and you throw up have diarrhea hot and cold sweats and food is out of the question by the second day you bones ache so bad you can hardly move in combination with the 1st day symptoms and no amount of cigarettes , booze or anything can help you and you slip into this writhing , squirming little worm of misery everything hurts even talking by the 3rd day your skin is on fire you have trouble breathing your nose is raw your butthole is raw your sweating thru the sheets but can't sleep you literally flop around on the bed like a fish out of water with no control I can remember praying to god please just kill me I can't take this anymore it hurts to breathe it hurts to move and you literally just lay in the fetal position waiting to die and convinced that you will at any moment. However if you can make it thru the 3rd day then you start to turn you still have aches and pains food doesn't look good and the color in your world takes on a new hue not so vibrant as when the opiates had ruled your life. You start to suffer that remorse, depression and feeling of hopelessness and hope all at the same time AND swear you will never get back on it! But the anxiety would always get me like how am I going to eat, sleep or go to work, function without it? So if you know where to get it then you almost always fall back in its vile little trap with the justification that this time you won't get strung out I'll just do 20 a day or whatever you think you can do without picking up your habit which by the way is consummated by using for 3 days. I would always joke with god why did you give us a 7 day week when you know its 3 days to kick and 3 days to get it back and you know us heroin addicts can't go 4 days off and 3 days on we always go 4 days on and then BOOM right back to where we started. So anyway this is the ridiculous cycle of hell most addicts go thru on a continuous basis and I was no different. Now don't get me wrong I was still trying to get sober in fact I rarely missed a day of going to meetings the only challenge was that I couldn't share because I was still addicted to heroin but I was sober from booze so I thought I was doing ok? Finally after a couple months I got my 3rd sponsor who I really identified with he was a guitar player who had used to live down on the pier in Santa Monica playing guitar for his drink money you know the type they still sit down there and do it today in pretty much every beach city in America or at least California. Anyway he had over 10 years sober and we liked music and he knew the feeling of desperation so I joined up with him and felt some new hope! He was a great guy and got me into the steps in a way I could understand but I was still doing heroin and he didn't know about that and also didn't have any experience in that area so I was able to convince him I was doing great and I even took sobriety coins but never showed anyone else because everyone else thought I had been sober for a while now and I was still taking 24hr chips and 30 days chip[s months after I told ruby I had been sober. So the wedding was finally approaching and I had failed once again in the getting clean dept. So I did the next best thing I had one of my best friends who had been sober for over a decade and also was a road manager for some of the most successful and crazy heavy metal bands in the world come stay with me as my roommate for the wedding and I hired my sponsor and his band to play the wedding reception so I thought I was pretty well surrounded and at least wouldn't drink during the whole weekend. Everyone was coming to this wedding relatives from both sides, friends, all the family over a 150 people total to the Madonna inn the weekend before Halloween 2001 and just a month after 9-11 so security in the airports was a nightmare for most of them. On the Friday before the wedding we each had things to do so we decided to meet up at the hotel that afternoon because we had to greet everyone and get ready for this amazing rehearsal party our friends and family had put together for us. So I called Rambo and said I coming to meet you and he said something that he never said No mas mi amigo. I was like what?!!!! Dude I'm getting married I need like 40 ballons to last me thru the weekend! He said maybe at 2pm call him back. So what am I supposed to do? I'm supposed to be in San Luis Obispo 3 hours north by 2pm. So I kept calling him back every hour and driving around east LA trying to cop from other people but NOBODY had anything and there was no way I could go without it. So this is what happened at 430 he calls me ok I got it but I could only get you 15! So I picked it up and knew I was in BIG trouble Ruby had been calling me and she was pissed I lied and said I was stuck in traffic which worked for a while until people that had left from LAX after me were already getting there I finally pulled in at 730 and everyone just looked at me and I knew what they were thinking but I just pulled out my charm went to my room spent 15 minutes getting high and came out to this amazing party where our friends and family had put together this cool themed event see the Madonna inn has themed rooms everything from love bird suite to jungle room and they had a 10 room themed party all set up we were greasers in one room with ice cream sodas to a disco room to Tarzan and Jane in a jungle room what a blast I had to keep ducking out to get high every hour but I think it worked out. I was feeling like the world was about to come crashing down at any moment though and felt like shit for holding everything up but I had to get dope right? So the day was finally here wedding day and lucky for me I had what I needed so after an hour long shower getting high I learned how to tie my 1st tie from my dad who was also the pastor for the wedding and when ruby came down a spiral staircase to earth angel I lost my mind and everything else disappeared and I knew that I would get clean and we would make it work! But 1st I had to go back to the room you know. So the reception was great we danced and had a great grooms cake made by our friend dahlia which looked just like my Gibson thunderbird bass guitar cake! Lucky I also had some Tina that night for the wedding night so I could perform sexually although with ruby it was never a problem even till the bitter end she was my dream date.

But now that the wedding was over we were to embark on the honeymoon! Now for most people being on their honeymoon it's the greatest time of the marriage new beginnings a week of just naked frolicking on a romantic beach somewhere? Those people aren't heroin addicts. We were also headed to Costa Rica clear across the world so For me the honeymoon was a pure anxiety attack because this was the October just after 9-11 and airport security was at an all-time high and I was at an all-time dependency on heroin so not only did I have to spend more than ½ the day before we left running all over town because Rambo was still out from the last time I saw him to score enough drugs but the morning before we left I had to swallow 17 balloons of heroin for our week long trip. I thought that would be enough BIG MISTAKE. So 1st off if your ever swallowed a large amount of drugs such as heroin for a cross country trip then you know what I am describing here if you haven't then consider yourself lucky! Going thru the machines was ok because they had yet to get the body x-ray machines in it was still just metal detectors but the challenge was then not exploding in my stomach and killing me which I was convinced was happening every time we hit a turbulence the second and more important challenge was keeping the ballons in my body till I could get to a safe place to um let's just say relieve them from their exit hole. Now obviously I was going to get dope sick long before we got to our destination so this was really freaking me out and I almost lost it going thru customs but we finally made it thru the trip to our destination and I was relieved. The only problem now was that they weren't coming out and it took a full 24 hrs. after we got there for the 1st couple to exit my body and by this time I was sick like flu sick but trying to put on a brave face while my beautiful bride dressed up in sexy outfits I lay there like a sack of potatoes unable to barely breathe little lone be the tommy lee /pam Anderson sex tape type of exotic lover that she was aching for. Now you probably think this is as humiliating as it gets right? I mean a diarrhea laden lover living off pepto bismol and cigarettes on your honey moon but it gets worse much worse so like I said 24 hrs. after we got there my little pellets of solution were popping out of my butt however I had nothing to do it with no spoons, no foil , so while we were at breakfast one morning I went to the kitchen and asked for an extra spoon and some foil and they were looking at me like yea buddy come on? Anyway I had stashed my dope in the bathrobe I was wearing and stuffed it under the bed so no one would find it but guess what while we were at breakfast the maid came in and shoved all of our towels and bathrobes in a non-descript white laundry bag and when I came back to find this I freaked out! I ran out of our room and find her in the next set of condo's over because we were at a very nice resort of course and said hey "where's my laundry?" I had some really important medicine in there! She didn't speak any English and just pointed to a pile of about 10-15 bags in the middle of the sidewalk out front my heart just sank because not only did I have no idea which bag was mine but it was out in plain view for everyone and their family to see this tattooed punk rocker going thru everyone's dirty laundry sweaty and sick but I found it and you would have thought I won the lottery! Of course ruby was like what are you doing?!! I just said I had some money or something in my bath robe I had to get it back then I went into the bathroom and tried to get well. The foil I borrowed was not like American foil so that didn't work so I ended up putting it in the spoon cooking it up and drinking it like soup which meant I didn't really get high and I ran out in 3 days of our 7 day stay also only about 12 ballons came out then and only 14 came out total I have no idea what happened to the other 2 or 3 I swallowed but I hope they don't find their way out now! So what's a dope fiend supposed to do when they run out of dope 3 days into a 7 day stay? What else become so miserable that staying there is a drag and come up with an elaborate plan to vacate the island in search of a better plan? Luckily it was hurricane season in Costa Rica so that helped because it literally rained cats, dogs and cows during our stay so it wasn't that hard to convince ruby to change our plans and go to the states we decided on New Orleans because it was romantic and had what I needed I thought. So we set off down these roads that were all but washed out it was a white knuckle 5 hour trip to the airport but I was determined to get us out of there because I was already getting sick again. We made it thru customs although at the airport a German Shepard drug dog stood up on my back walking thru our line up I always wondered if he smelt it on me or thru me. Either way the customs guy took a look at me and decided it wasn't worth it and let us keep on going (once again god was looking out for me because I knew there were still at least 2 or 3 balloons inside of me that hadn't come out and I didn't want them coming out in a toilet in a 3rd world country!)So we made it to New Orleans and settled in then I ended the marriage before it even had gotten started. What happened wasn't planned it never is right? But anyway I went out to a Mexican restaurant while ruby got ready for our big night out on the town carriage ride, fancy restaurant walking hand in hand thru the streets of the big easy loving and living our beautiful life. Anyway so I went to a restaurant called Nacho mama's off Decatur see I was so driven to find heroin I even thought a Mexican restaurant would have someone in it that could help me I was desperate! So while I sat at the bar eating some tacos I decided why not have a beer? I thought one Coors light isn't going to do anything right? So I ordered one the woman told me it was happy hour buy one get one free! Damn Nawlins such a giving city. So 1 turned into 2 to 3 to 4 then a rockabilly band showed up to play and I told them I play stand-up bass too so they suggested I sit in. I was watching the clock it was 430 and I had to be back by 6 for our date so I said sure next thing I know we are taking buy 1 get one free tequila shots when I got up the courage to ask for some dope. The singer seemed the most likely to have some so I asked him he was like no but you want to get stoned I got some great weed. I said ok why not I needed to quit drinking cause I was already 6 Coors lts and 2 tequila shots in and I thought it would mellow me out so we went outside to smoke well he was wasn't that good so we smoked 3 joints of it and it was the creeper and it hit me about 15 minutes later now at this point I am rocking out having fun and I don't notice that it is already 630 and I'm late so I bailed. When I walked into the room ruby was in this beautiful bride style rock n roll outfit ready to go but I was wasted I blurted out going to take a shower then we can go and she said your fucking slurring your words your drunk!! I tried to lie but it was no use because I was wasted this was one of the most hurtful things I had ever done such a selfish, egotistical move on my part she burst into tears and cancelled the evening no matter what I said she just lay there crying. I took a shower and got ready and she was not having it so I did something different I went to a payphone and started calling people I knew from AA back in LA finally a woman picked up the phone I didn't know her that well and she pretty much told me to get to a meeting and not drink anymore but come on I'm in New Orleans and already drunk so it's not stopping! So on my own I went from bar to bar down one side of bourbon street to the other but nothing could get ready of my shame that night I finally went to rallies and got some burgers and went back to the room ruby didn't even acknowledge me when I got back and I passed out worthless and hopeless I knew then I could not stop on my own and I was scared to death of how bad it was going to get before I figured out how to get the help I needed.

Houston we have a Problem

So back home to LA we went and things got a little bit better but then came the day when the bill for the wedding came back unpaid and ruby asked did I know about the missing money? I had been taking a little off the top for a while but hadn't realized that thousands of dollars had gone to my dope habit see I had every good intention of paying it back but still hadn't gotten a job yet and then it all hit the fan and once again she gave me the ultimatum shape up or you're getting shipped out and I promised for the millionth time I'm good now don't worry. We made it to the weekend of my birthday march 15th 6 months almost to the day that we had gotten married when I finally blew it beyond repair. It started on march 14th when we went to Tony Hawk's Birthday party since Ruby worked with Tony on some stuff we were invited and I promised to behave myself and I did but A dry drunk is even worse than a drunk in my opinion. I sat there all night watching everyone just get wasted this was during the tony hawk pro skater video days and jack ass fame so there was a lot of drinking tenacious D was playing it was just a shit show and I sat there like a boiling pot of water on slow simmer. But we finally made it out and went home. The next morning I was up earlier than normal because it was my birthday and I wanted to do fun stuff! I have always loved my birthday and have also committed the worst relapses on my birthday but I'm getting ahead of my story. So ruby was hung-over and wanted to sleep so I decided to go to an AA meeting get my head on straight but on the way to the meeting my fucked up head convinced me it was my birthday and since I wasn't drinking I should go get a couple of balloons down in east LA no one would know right? So I drove down there and bought 6. I went back home stuck my head in the door told ruby I had a great meeting I was feeling better and for her to sleep as long as she wanted I was going to play some bass in the garage. Well I was in the garage getting high when all of a sudden the door flew open I had always locked the door but that morning I had forgotten and in she walked in a cute little sexy lingerie outfit with my birthday cake complete with sparklers for candles singing happy birthday then she saw me with a plate of dope in front of me I blurted out what I always said " it's not what it looks like" but of course it was and that was it she threw the cake at me and let out a primal scream that I have come to know over the years as the complete breaking of a heart or the sound of ultimate suffering mostly I hear it from parents who have lost their kids to drugs or getting shot but on that day it was my wife that made that sound and I knew I was done. She screamed get out of my house! It was no longer our house and I knew that she had finally had it. For 7 years she had watched me struggle she had backed me up, she had stood up for me when others said I was a junky, she had given her heart and soul to a man that could not get clean and sober and she was finally incapable of giving anymore of her heart or soul to this obvious hopeless case. So I got out I took some more money and did the only thing I knew to do went and scored more heroin and went to my crystal dealer's house to get as numb as possible. Now I thought this was going to be a temporary situation and she would let me back in the house after a week or so but that didn't happen. So I went from staying at friends' houses while they would let me but after a couple of weeks I had lost a job with my then brother in law but ended up getting hired at trader joes the one right by our house. I had applied 3 months before but they had finally just called so I thought she would take me back nope. She actually filed an annulment to get rid of any record of the marriage. So I was living in my car at this point staying in Hollywood scoring in downtown LA and working in Santa Monica which was tough. Then one day I needed money and she came to the car to give it to me and I'll never forget the look she gave me when she broke into tears I have never still to this day seen anyone with such a look of sadness combined with disgust she tossed the money at me and ran down the street crying and that was one of the last times I would see her. Then the parking tickets got to be so much I had to give her back the car so I lived just on the street and I would still try and make it to work at 5 am on the bus but it didn't always work out plus at lunch I would borrow coworkers cars to race into east LA and cop dope and try to get back but I was always late and people would say my car smells weird what did you eat for lunch? LOL so eventually I got fired from that job too. Now this is when it gets really pathetic I had no car, no home I was strung out and this is how I lived sleeping in parks off Hollywood Blvd. or on the church steps of a church on Highland and La Brea. I sold crack for a while but that didn't work out I hated crack and the people I had to deal with at the time. I would steal t shirts off those tourists' stores on Hollywood Blvd so I didn't look homeless and I would use gas station bathrooms or fast food bathrooms every morning I always had a spare quarter for these emergencies. So I would shave and take bird baths so I wasn't completely homeless looking put on my new stolen shirt and face the day then I would call everyone I knew to borrow money or I would steal stuff like Cd's or porno mags from this store on Hollywood Blvd. to re sell to a guy who owned q liquor store and would buy anything from homeless people or trade us in malt liquor either was ok for me as long as I got something. Then I would go buy Davis's house and get some crystal if he was around or if I had dope money I would head to east LA to get that. I remember one day I was really sick and needed some dope so I stole a bike and began the 10 mile ride to east LA from Hollywood. As I was going down Cahuenga full speed this guy opened up his truck door and nailed me I flew into the middle of traffic and thought I was dead for sure but once again god had my back. He came over and said are you ok? I was thinking in my head what to do and so I said yea I'm ok but I was supposed to go meet a friend for lunch and now my phone is broke and my bike is mangled can you give me a ride? Now let me paint the picture I was laying in the middle of the street the front tire was bent in half, the chain was broken, my ribs were broken and my leg was completely shredded and bleeding but I needed my dope man! He was like sure man I will give you a ride. So I'm giving this guy directions and he starts going are you sure this is the right way? Cause see I copped in the east LA where no white people went but we finally got there and it was a video store front but they sold heroin not DVD's. So we parked and I told him I'll be right back he asked if I smoked cigarettes I said yea camel lights so while I went into the video store he went into the liquor store across the parking lot. When I got back to his truck he had a case of heineken and a carton of camels waiting for me then he gave me a ride to a friend's house where I was staying. I'll never forget this I mean this guy was so nice and grateful I wasn't dead or going to sue him but I just wanted to get high man. I got to my friend's house and he opened the door and I'll never forget that look I'm standing there with a bike mangled blood fresh up and down my leg holding a case of beer and a carton of cigarettes with a big smile on my face hey bro I said as I walked in. Now see in my mind this was a great day I mean I always had to pay a price to get my dope and this day was no different but he was appalled and said we need to take you to the hospital dude. I was like no I'm good and I proceeded to drink my beer and do my dope but about 8 o clock that night I was running out of stuff and was in a lot of pain so I asked him to take me to the hospital I was thinking do it now and I can get some pain pills right? But after x-rays they asked what insurance I had and I had none so he told me my arms was not broken but the bone was bent I had 3 broken ribs and my leg would take about 2 weeks to heal but that was it no pills I was so pissed! My arm is still crooked but at least I didn't die that day. Just another day in the life of a junky. I still have a divet in my forearm where the door hit me. Now I want to paint a realistic version of being homeless for those of you who don't know what it is like. I would spend the day just trying to survive the conditions and there was no peace what so ever because I had no shelter , no food , no place to even go to the bathroom you don't realize how much you miss being able to take a shit in peace until you have no bathroom and you can't just eat when you hungry you have to either beg money off people collect cans and bottles then drag them thru the streets to a recycling center (so humiliating) to wait in line cash in your ticket and then go buy whatever you can afford. Now I realize that a lot of my own personal decisions led me to this and I take full responsibility for that but I also know that my addiction wasn't me thinking clearly or more importantly it allowed me to be in this situation and for me to believe I deserved all of this calamity with is even harder to deal with once you get clean the whole I've done so many bad things I can never get any life back that is decent. But getting ahead of my story again so my day would start off and any time of the day because night and day are the same when you are homeless night is usually your day because you don't want to go to sleep for fear of what will get you either someone attacking you or the police arresting you so sleep is never peaceful just as a necessity. Then I would cruise the streets getting whatever I needed to get drunk or high to numb myself and my situation. I would gather cigarette butts off the ground or out of those gravel filled ashtrays outside of grocery stores so at least I could smoke and I remember to this day the embarrassment of seeing someone see me do this and the look of disgust they would give me. I ate 2 different ways at night I would wait for restaurants to close and for them to take out the trash then I would raid the dumpsters seeing what was salvageable pizza places were always good for something or I would go into the grocery store and pretend to shop and I would order things from the deli like chicken wings something I could eat in a bite or 2 then as I walked around I would eat my wings or bulk granola and toss the sack behind the dog food or something where no other food was this is also how I would get my day drinks because I would take those club cocktail drinks and guzzle them while I was walking down the aisle. Then I would put some malt liquor cans in my backpack with some more bulk food bags of nuts or chocolate covered pretzels and then go to the frozen food section and but those Resers frozen burritos for 25 cents drop my basket leave the other food items put my burrito up on the conveyor belt and pay my 25 cents so it looked like I bought something at least. Pathetic I know but it was all I knew to do and how I never got caught I can only thank god for letting me escape from that hell. Now being a heroin addict doesn't really make you hungry so this wasn't the only focus I had and sometimes when the heat would get to hot in the store and the security guard started following me I would go to McDonald's where cheeseburgers were only 39 cents or hamburgers were only 29 cents I would buy 2 then go to a Latino market off highland ave and buy 25 cent bag of chips and my breakfast would be one burger ½ the chips and for dinner I would eat the other burger and chips. To put this in perspective I was spending all my money on drugs and alcohol as least 25 dollars or more a day on that. There were good days and bad days but the weekends were the toughest because then Hollywood was packed with tourists from all over and I could never find a place to sleep or rest without being harassed mostly I would go hang out in abandoned buildings or empty office buildings were good to break into as well but I was always scared to death of getting caught so usually I would just walk the streets hour after hour day after day trying to avoid mirrors or people so I didn't have to see what I looked like or how they looked at me. Sometimes on the weekend nights I would get cleaned up and go to bars where there was no cover places like the frolic room or burgundy room and try and meet some woman who would rescue me but that never worked out and usually when the bar closed I would be broke and alone once again. Then I would go to the all night dance clubs and stand outside trying to catch someone's eye to rescue me but that never happened either so I just kept walking up and down Hollywood Blvd looking to make friends with other broken toys who called the Blvd home. Sunday mornings were always the worst because Saturday nights would be just chaotic with drunken people everywhere but on Sunday morning around 6am when the sun came up the trash the quiet and the stench of debauchery always made me think of that song by Johnny Cash Sunday morning coming down and pretty much every Sunday morning with tears in my eyes I wondered how much longer I could put up the fight? Finally after almost 9 months of this I broke in a parking lot of ralphs on 3rd and La Brea I went to give another homeless guy a dollar I owed him after we had just cashed that days' supply of bottles and cans and he said to me it's cool Chris you keep it you need it worse than me! OMG I was outraged how dare this old hobo not take my money and say that to me then as I walked down La Brea Blvd I looked in a store window and saw someone I didn't recognize anymore if fact I thought someone was standing next to me and when I turned to talk to them I realized it was me and I just started to cry I was done and it was only 9 am on a Tuesday and there was no amount of drugs or alcohol I could put in my body to make this pain go away and I decided I needed to take action So the next morning at 645am I stood in line with the other homeless people waiting to get into the Hollywood library to use one of the 10 computers you could rent for 30 minutes. I was 7th in line and made the cut. I sent an email to my savior my sister and explained my situation my time was up and so I left not knowing what was to become of me. The next day at 645am I was back in line waiting to use the computer I was sick, broke and miserable and when I sat down to open up my email I prayed to god again please let her reply and when I opened up the email she had replied and said she could help then she gave a list of rules I would have to follow or the deal was off immediately. I agreed and felt a sigh of relief but I was still on the streets and wouldn't rest until I got out to where she lived in Arlington VA a whole world away to me. The next day she sent money for a motel for me to stay in until my flight left on Saturday morning. Now this is how sick the addicts mind worked on Friday night I had my suitcase with all I owned packed up and ready to go but I couldn't sleep so at 5am with a 9am flight pending and with cab money in my pocket for the trip to the airport and my freedom I decided to go downtown one more time so I grabbed a train and went to 6th and Alvarado where all the dealers hung out but no one was there? So I kept walking around and found a guy in an area I didn't really trust but I was desperate so with 40 of my last 50 bucks I bought 6 balloons I got back to the motel at 645 opened my balloons and found out I had been ripped off no dope just brown sugar! So now I had an hour to get to the airport and only 10 bucks I called everyone I could think of and finally found a Mexican taxi who would take me for the ten bucks I made it to the airport at 8am broke , sick, and disgusted which is the only way I would leave anything in my life goodbye Hollywood I said good riddance got on the plane and fell asleep finally fuck this place I said under my breath since I was 16 years old that town trained me like a pet monkey and never gave me the banana it was time to join a new circus!

Rising Up from the Ashes

There's always a 1st time of success for addicts sometimes it's a week sometimes a month or more? Well this was my 1st time actually getting some success when I got off that plane to meet my sister and brother in law I was wearing a grey sharkskin suit and a maroon button up shirt and the 1st thing she said was wow we expected much worse from your email and once again I had dressed up my outsides so the world wouldn't know how bad my insides were messed up and how broken I was on the inside. I arrived on a Saturday night and we went to a friend of theirs for dinner so there wasn't much time to discuss my predicament but the next day it was laid out like this I had basically 3 days to get a job any job, I had screwed up my life and I had no excuses left and no amount of justification on my situation I had lost a home, a beautiful wife, my self-respect and pretty much everything I had owned and it was time to face the music and I did. This is also where I finally had a chance to feel safe and address my alcoholism and addiction in a loving environment. I went to my 1st AA meeting that Sunday night at a hospital in Arlington VA and for the 1st time I felt some hope and I met my 1st sponsor on the east coast I left there ecstatic that maybe I was going to finally be able to change my life had I been humbled enough? When I got home that night and crawled into my nieces bed since I was staying in her room while she slept in another room I looked at the holly hobby sheets and at 31 years old finally thanked god that I was still alive and that I finally had 36 hours of being COMPLETELY sober for the 1st time in over 15 years. The next day I hit the job path hard and by that afternoon I had a very promising job as a server at of all places Rock Bottom Brewery LOL that's the irony and the way god kept me in check. I can be very charming when I want but that day I just looked the manager in the eye and begged for a chance. I passed the online personality test and was hired the next day! My life got better real quick by going to meetings and working as much as possible but I still hadn't done my steps and I got into some relationships that I probably shouldn't have but I stayed sober and then I got my second sponsor who got me thru steps 1-5 so I thought I was cured and because of my 1st sponsor I was actively involved with the fire department which is what I decided would be my next career. I had made it thru Thanksgiving, Christmas and my birthday on march 15th sober as a judge and had even been a huge part of my rock bottoms Christmas outreach to a halfway house which was kind of weird because I knew some of the people who lived there from AA meetings. I also had made some friends that are still my friends today my friends Cam, Molly and Lindsay were all big supporters and my friends Tom and Beth from the goon house a punk rock house in Arlington hung out with me and went to rock shows together. My friend Tom died from addiction years later and Beth is like clean like me and just celebrated 5 years. Cam and Molly ended up getting married and Lindsay is the most successful woman that I know and a true friend still to this day. I also met quite a few firefighters and EMT/Paramedics who became my friends especially 2 guys named Jason and Bill firefighters from D.C. and Fairfax Co respectfully. I had just celebrated 6 months when Jason asked if I was serious about becoming a firefighter and I said yes so he said they had an opening in their house for a roommate but you had to be a firefighter to live there or at least becoming one so I said that would be awesome! I went home and asked my sister if it was ok if I moved in with those guys I mean I had a job and 6 months of sobriety , a sponsor I mean I was doing great and she agreed she even gave me one of her cars to use till I could buy one of my own. So on a Saturday morning I put my clothes in the car and drive the mile and a half from my sister's house to my new place ready to take on the world become a firefighter, get married and put my old life behind me! I walked in put my clothes down on the bed and went to the bathroom to take a leak and out of habit I opened the medicine cabinet and there I saw a bottle of Vicodin I did the math and realized they had had this bottle for 27 days and only taken 2 pills so I thought I'm doing so good what could a couple of Vicodin do and they won't even miss them so I popped 3 right away and I couldn't believe it I hadn't even put my clothes away and already I had ruined 6 months of sobriety where was my will power? Where was the remembrance of being fucking homeless barely 6 months ago and all that my sister had done for me? All the stuff went out the window and within 4 days that bottle was gone and I had started drinking beer again only miller light but still I was no longer sober and I would see any more sobriety for longer than a month for quite a few years. Now I still was going to AA it's not like I just gave up and things kept getting better I got a transfer and promotion to another job thru rock bottom and I became the banquet coordinator of their District Chophouse location in DC and I started making real money enough to travel all over the country taking firefighter tests everywhere from Las Vegas to Charlotte NC, Orange County CA where even at 35 years old and a former heroin addict at this point I came in in the top 10 of the Cpat or physical test out of over 100 applicants so I thought I was invincible! I was drinking on the daily again and mixing weed and cocaine with it but still holding it together I mean I knew everyone and was a community leader with my job I even got to meet Mayor Marion Barry one day at an event he was a good guy to me and we had a good talk that day both of us were probably 2 sheets to the wind but still it was where I was at in life and when you're talking to the mayor life can't be all bad. I had a girlfriend at this time her name was peaches and she kept me in line most of the time and would get me thru a lot of my black tie events and her heart was pure like a little girl she loved me unconditional but eventually she moved to Boston and moved on with her life she is one of only 2 girlfriends I have had in my life that I still don't have any contact with to this day but peaches if you read this thank you for loving me thru some tough stuff. So at this point I had graduated from EMT school and was just waiting for the call to get hired on at a fire dept. I was completely out of AA at this point and was hanging out with some hard partying punk rock kids and having a lot of fun I had money a killer truck which I nicknamed the #1 Hollywood and I would grab Beth or some of my other friends and we would hit Baltimore to see LA Guns or I would go with my friend Jessica to see Rancid or the epic shows with Jason my roommate going to see the Dropkick Murphy's talk about getting hammered! I loved DC for that coming from LA it was always hard to see shows or park etc. but in DC man it was like just show up and park and walk in. Since I worked downtown DC I also had complete access to the MCI center for Capitals games and even became friends with Alex Ovechkin and his parents for a while. I mean come on how could I be an alcoholic with all of this awesomeness going on? My drinking was not only daily now but I felt like I was invincible I worked in a bar I attended charity gala's in my tuxedo and then one night it all came crashing down. The night started out like any other I was bartending at the chophouse with my friend Rich and we were hitting it pretty hard it was a Friday and that meant that my coke dealer was coming in to hook me up like he did every Friday night so I knew I could drink as much as I wanted around 9 I had already had about 4 or 5 beers and 3 shots of tuaca an Italian liquor about 3 vodka red bulls and snorted 3 or 4 lines of coke so I was feeling no pain and still pretty much in control. Then my friend georgette came in now I had a huge crush on her and had been trying to get her to go out with me for months now and on that night she asked me to come meet her after work at a bar up the street! I couldn't wait so after work about 2 hours later I walked out of my job and it was pouring so instead of walking the 3 blocks to the other bar I decided to walk a block to my truck and then drive up to meet her so I wouldn't get wet and ruin my clothes and hair. The ego has a wicked way of making us do things that when we look back we go why on earth would I have done that? But I was on a mission so after all those drinks and a couple of shots more I snorted the last of my coke about a quarter gram cranked up some ac/dc and headed out. Now how I thought I could find parking in downtown DC on a Friday night still remains a mystery to me but I thought I could. After driving around for about 15 minutes I started to get irritated and it was raining even harder so I could barely see so I took a right hand turn on my green light not really paying attention and then I heard this really loud thump! I looked behind me thru my window I had a 2004 lifted ford f150 at the time and saw a large African American man in a black trench coat flipping me off and shaking his fist at me? I thought he was just a homeless guy and I thought it was weird but I was in a hurry so I just kept driving then about a block after that I decided I should go back and see what had happened so as I rounded the next block 3 FBI cops raced down the street and boxed me in. The 1st cop came up and had me roll down the window and asked me what I was doing? I said going home he asked where do you live I said Arlington he pointed the opposite direction of where I was headed and said Arlington is that way then he said have you been drinking? I said no sir then I pointed to my firefighter stickers on my back windshield and said I'm a firefighter officer I wouldn't do that. Then he asked again have you been drinking I said well I did have a beer with my dinner about 3 hours ago but that's it. I felt confident in this answer because I had gum in and had just done enough coke to traumatize a small horse so I didn't think I looked or sounded drunk. He asked a 3rd time Chris have you been drinking I said again I had a beer with dinner and I'm a firefighter so what is the problem? Then he said Chris you have lied to me since I started asking you questions you said you were going home but you're driving in the opposite direction I asked if you had been drinking you said no but I am standing a foot and a half away from you and can smell the booze on your breath so do you want to tell me the truth? I said ok you got me officer I have been drinking but I'm not drunk I'm a firefighter so I'll just pull over and get my truck tomorrow sorry for any inconvenience. He said well if you're not drunk then let's do a field sobriety test you should be able to pass no problem and I said yea let's do that. Cocky and stupid! So after 15 minutes of tests he said ok stand up against the wall and put your hands above your head I said for what? He said cause I'm taking you in for a DUI I said you can't do that I'm a firefighter and this will make me lose any chance of being a firefighter you don't know what I've been thru pleading and then I told him how I'd been a heroin addict and homeless and how I was just getting back on my feet and this would destroy everything. He told me to look over my shoulder and when I did I saw that African American guy in the trench coat then the cop said to me if I could let you go Chris I would but that is a captain of the north Carolina highway patrol who is in town for a fallen policemen vigil tonight his brother was killed in the line of duty 2 years ago by a drunk driver and he was walking back to his hotel tonight when he stepped off the curb to cross the street a truck almost ran him over the officer yelled stop and said he saw the driver look back and then keep on driving does any of this ring a bell? I went oh shit I knew I was screwed I said can I go talk to him? The cop said no he wants you taken in so I was arrested and charged with DUI I blew over 3 times the legal limit and hit and run on a police officer. I felt like my whole world had just stopped and I was going to prison for a long time. They took me to the federal building in DC and booked me I called some friends who were lawyers and they called the head of the law office who must have had some pull because by 5 am I was a free man at least from jail so I did what every alcoholic does I took a cab to the closest liquor store that opened at 6am bought some beer and when home and started drinking nothing could stop me not even the thought of 10 years plus in prison. When I got home I saw that georgette had called like 10 times so I called her and told her what happened and I never got that date because I was not allowed back in the city of DC for quite some time. Now the silver lining was that I didn't get booked in DC city jail or I might still be there today.

Also my lawyer was a very prominent man in DC and we postponed the case for over a year and also my sponsor at the time was a decorated firefighter who knew the cop so besides losing any chance of being a firefighter I actually never went to prison and just lost my license for 6 months but only in DC so I could still drive in VA which is where I lived. The final thing that god helped me with is that even though I had a felony it only showed up in DC so since I never lived there for every job or house I applied to it never showed up! God has always been keeping his hand on me. Now my drinking really got bad after that because I had no job and was depressed over not being able to achieve my dream once again. I was so bad I would actually wake up at 7 am to drink for 3 hours before going to a noon meeting to get my court card signed and then I would drink 2 gallons of water before I went to my DUI class and had to take a pee test. I never failed one but probably came very close a few times. Eventually I got a job at trader Joes even though I had been fired from the one in LA I talked them into hiring me again saying that I was young and made a lot of bad decisions but I had learned my lesson and it wouldn't happen again. Also around this time I would meet the 3rd love of my life her name was Rachel and we met at a Hatebreed and Exodus show on Labor Day 2005. From the minute I saw her I just knew she was gorgeous with fake boobs and she loved metal so she met all my requirements. She also had a good job and had a great sense of humor and we became the ultimate rock n roll couple in VA. WE did everything together and had each other's backs no matter what. The big bonus was that she had always wanted to move to southern CA and I really wanted to go home so that set the wheels in motion. But 1st there was drinking and rocking out to do and that we did best. I knew for sure she was the one for me when for Christmas 2 months after we met she got us tickets to see a twisted Christmas with twisted sister without me even telling her that dee snider was my favorite human well besides her. So the next couple of years were a blur of partying and we had a blast! Eventually I lost my job at trader Joes I had been helping myself to wine tastings daily and I had pretty much tasted every bottle of wine we sold and one day I decided to help myself to some other stuff and got caught it was a stupid thing to do because I really liked working there and the people I worked with but I was a selfish ego driven alcoholic with no regard to others property or respect for them it is what we call in alcoholics anonymous a self will run riot and so I paid the price. Now I also never put my drinking on anyone else so Rachel had no part in any of my stealing or by being drunk at work every day and I know she would not have approved of any of it but I never told her and was a great manipulator and liar I always had an excuse of why life had wronged me. Eventually I had also gotten kicked out of the house I lived in with my firefighter friends and was living with Rachel in the basement of one of my mom's friends' houses and I was so grateful for that because I couldn't handle all the responsibility of paying bills, my credit was shot and so this seemed ok at the time but I also felt like a real dirt bag every week when the recycling went out and it was packed with all my empty bottles in fact quite a few times I would take garbage bags of bottles down the street to a dumpster instead of face the humiliation of carrying them up to the bin we shared. I also got a job working under the table for a fire inspection company which really enabled me to start drinking all day. My job was basically to go into businesses and re tag fire extinguishers or take the expired ones back to the shop and re fill them so I could just do whatever I wanted as long as the jobs got done and there were plenty of days when I would go into the shop pick up my work orders and then come home take a couple hour nap to get over my hangover and then make up some excuse about being stuck in traffic so the jobs did not get done. That or I would come in and go back home drink a couple beers and smoke some weed to get over my hangover and then go to work. I pretty much worked 4 hours a day and drank the rest and life was good but I was quickly becoming a man I hated unreliable and my dreams were so far away I was suffocating in mediocrity and knew that Rachel wasn't as enthused in my new choices as she was when I had been a budding firefighter or store manager or even thinking about getting the band back together instead of a portly couch potato only interested in drinking and drugging my life away. So we decided that a change of scenery would be a great cure so we took a trip to San Diego/LA and of course hanging with my old rock star pals partying the night away at the rainbow and in Hollywood seemed like the perfect remedy so we decided to move out to CA but the only problem was it was so expensive and Rachel's family all lived in VA and as much as she wanted to move I also know she struggled with leaving her family. But instead of moving to CA we decided why not move to Vegas instead it was a lot cheaper and both of us had friends there and were told jobs were waiting for us so we decided to move to Vegas just for a year then head to CA. Now this is of course looking back seems like the worst decision ever! I mean if you have read this book at all so far why on earth would anyone support me in this decision yea let's take the alcoholic/addict to Vegas and start a new life! Completely absurd but like I said before I was a master manipulator and nobody could tell me anything anyway. But I did want a new life and wanted to show Rachel I was serious about creating these dreams and a life together so before we moved I took her to our favorite restaurant in Georgetown called Filomenas and at the chefs table in a private area I popped the question and she said yes! So freshly engaged we had a new sense of hope plus now there was a reason to celebrate and that we did. Looking back now I realize that wasn't the right move as much as I loved her I really was scared of being all alone and drinking myself to death so I wanted a commitment that she wouldn't leave me when it got ugly which it was destined to do and for all the bullshit I put her thru I am still to this day truly sorry. But the show must go on and at the time I didn't see myself as a liability but rather a visionary intent on making dreams possible.

Sin City Here We Come

We drove across country from Arlington to Vegas taking a week and going to New Orleans, Graceland and some other places and finally came to Vegas ready to rock! We stayed with our friends April and Asher and within 3 days found an apt on of all places Paradise rd. in Vegas or Henderson with a great BBQ place down the street and in the same area as all of our friends I got a job waiting tables and she got a job working at a title office and things were great we were definitely Vegas types drinking and drugging almost every night well at least I was she wasn't like that and she could just party on the weekends but not me I lived for the party and I started hanging out with people who shared my enthusiasm. It wasn't long till I got fired from my 1st job but picked up a second job right away which is where the real trouble started for 2 reasons A I met a pill connection who had laura tabs and oxy and I was making good money so I could afford it. It still had not become a problem yet and we were still having a blast I remember our 1st thanksgiving we decided to get a wii game console and got some insider info that they were coming in on a Sunday morning so we stayed out drinking all night went to target at 2am met some fellow partyers and with only 100 available we were 94th in line and we got one that was epic and the couple we met had booze I had some coke so we had the time of our lives of course by the time we got the wii and got home we were thoroughly wasted! But it was a fun time. The more I got into pills the more our relationship suffered I was more angry all the time we had separate hours she worked days I worked night so it was tough to spend any none party time together but we still tried .Eventually I met the connect and from then on I was using oxy daily I was never without pills and was actually dependent on them. That's when things began to unravel between us we had never fought before and now we argued almost every day and unless we were wasted we really didn't do anything together. This was also one of the 1st times since we active heroin addiction that my body started to give out. I had developed an enlarged liver and stomach problems and my daily routine was pretty much wake up take 2 or 3 lorotabs500 mg then drink 2 22oz beers then I would fill up a Gatorade bottle with vodka and sparks energy malt liquor drinks snort some coke smoke some weed and head to work. I would buy 3 or 4 airplane bottle of vodka to get me thru the day and usually bring some coke and more pills to get thru the night. Then after work I would really drink more beer shots of tuaca, bottles of wine my drink of choice for a long time was a 22oz icehouse, a fifth of vodka and a bottle of zinfandel all set up in front of me and I would just sit there and drink pop pills smoke weed and watch TV until I passed out. After about a year in Vegas we were in the urgent care for the 2nd time in as many weeks and the doctor was telling us that my drinking was killing me my liver had become enlarged and that if I didn't quit things would rapidly decline. Rachel told the doctor that she would make sure I didn't drink and that she wouldn't see us again that was on a Sunday. On Thursday night Rachel came to me and asked if we could go out since that was our normal deal I said no how could we I had only not drank for 3 days so why would I go to a bar and she said we can go you just have to drink which to most people would make sense but I am an alcoholic and I just can't not drink I told her that's like taking a kid to a candy store and then telling him he can't have any? Then why we would come to the candy store? So I told her go without me I'll just hang out thinking she would say no I'll stay here with you. Instead she took off and that pissed me off. I told myself she didn't care about me and that she was a hypocrite and a liar for what she told the Dr but the reality was that I had done whatever I wanted the whole time we had been together with no real regard to what she wanted so why shouldn't she do the same I'm sure all the times I had left her behind to go drinking had taken their effect on her as well. Now at this time I don't think she was looking for someone else but I mean how many times can you go to a bar and especially being as beautiful as she was not have guys hit on you, buy you drinks etc. before you find someone to hang out with and drink and laugh with especially when coming home meant hanging with a miserable drug addict and alcoholic trying to get sober? So as the days turned into weeks and the weeks turned into months I knew that she had found someone I also know that she was loyal during the time we were together but anyone that's human is going to be more attracted to someone who is fun than miserable so it wasn't that big of a surprise when she came home one day took off the ring and said I'm moving out so you can get your shit together I love you but I don't want to sit around and be with someone who has to be sober when I don't so I'm leaving. I was hurt of course but I also secretly was like yea go so I can start drinking again and have no one to be around so I can do whatever I want. I still had my job so I could barely afford the apt but it would be tough and I would need more drugs to accomplish my goals of powering thru. Now the loneliness I felt after she left was unbearable I had never felt so alone. Now I had tried one more time to get sober at this point and one night after drinking with our friends Rich and Kate I had asked Rich to help me he was and is one of my best friends and it was apparent I had lost the battle with booze so we made a deal he would come over every morning at 730 and pick me up and get me out of my house so I didn't wake up and start drinking because that was the only way I could accomplish this. So every morning he came over woke me up and we would go run errands or I would go to his work at an Irish pub and watch TV and drink diet Pepsi's till it was time for me to go to work then I would get off work and go home and try not to drink and at some point I had 30 days of not drinking but I was still taking pills so I wouldn't go into seizures from withdrawals and so I could make it thru work I took a 30 day chip and gave it to rich thanking him for saving my life. That chip would make a huge impact on my sobriety about a year later.

Can't Die but I'm Still Trying

So after Rachel moved out I lost my shit and started really doing pills and drinking again not caring about anything I even moved my dealer into my house so I could have 24 hr. access to my pills which at this time were Oxycontin and lauratabs, roxy's, Vicodin you name it plus I was back on the malt liquor and vodka from morning till night. This went on for months until one day when I was sitting on my couch it was a Sunday in the spring and I had woken up gone from my bed to the couch where I set up my drinks of choice and a plate with 5 or 6 oxy's and cocaine on it and I was just going to blur my day away. I remember my dealer had moved out because I was too much of a pest and would hound him constantly he also found a place to live for free and I had started charging him rent after he couldn't provide enough pills to keep me satisfied and I became greedy. I remember hearing kids playing outside at the pool in our apt complex and that just pissed me off because I couldn't stand the thought of people being happy while I was literally one step from deaths door. About 530 I had been sitting there for 5 hours constantly putting drugs and alcohol into my body and still able to feel emotions which I hated so I decided to up my intake I remember snorting a full 80 oxy these were the green ones you could still wipe the coating off and then crush up into powder form guzzling vodka straight out of the bottle opening a new bottle of wine and going I need more pills so I crushed up another 80 snorted half and then I remember my left leg going numb and I thought no biggie it's just falling asleep I've been sitting here all day I snorted the half and my right leg went numb then my left arm and I knew I had fucked up so I reached for my phone with my right hand that was the last thing I remember it was 620 pm on Sunday night the next thing I know I woke up on the floor of my living room with my phone in my hand and 911 on the screen it was dark so I thought it was still Sunday night but when I got up I looked at the TV and it was 9pm on Tuesday I had been unconscious for over 48hrs and had passed out before I could send the 911 call I had no idea why I was still alive but I got up from the floor looked at the table saw a pill on the plate and booze still in the vodka bottle so I sat down crushed up the pill snorted it and made myself a drink thinking to myself I am so far gone I can't stop even a near death experience couldn't make me stop even for 5 minutes after I got up off the floor and I began to cry. Thinking God why won't you just let me die dammit!! I can't take this anymore but he had other plans I guess. Eventually my lease was up and I had to move I wasn't making the money I had been because honestly I could barely make it thru an hour of sober time at this point so my tips and shifts had suffered. Some friends at my work were looking for a roommate and the place was nice and the price was perfect so I moved in. I decided at this point it was a fresh start so I enrolled in Culinary School and really wanted to get my life back on track. For a while I did really good I got down to ½ an oxy a day a couple of loratab and was only drinking beer I started school and things were looking up. However after a couple of months I couldn't stay at that level and because I had no tools to quit I ended up right back where I started and my habit had become an obsession one more time. Now this is where a couple of events started to really get me close to my bottom. I had given up on food at this point except for a jack in the box burger dipped in a plastic cup of malt liquor as my meal of the day if I smelled food I would gag so I had to cover it up with the beer to get it down. Then I was in school one day making burrata cheese with a very famous chef from the hard rock hotel when the obsession hit I literally told him I was going to the bathroom I walked out of class out of school and drove 30 minutes to get some oxy and never made it back. When I got home I sat down and just asked myself am I insane?!! I mean this chef was known as the rock n roll chef and I had been standing right next to him as a student he could have been my new best friend and helped me get into the coolest hotel in the world and I just walked out never to see him again or basically that school again because I couldn't face my classmates who were surely going to ask where did you go? Luckily it was almost Christmas break so I just called in sick for a couple days after telling one of my teachers I had some bad news from the Dr. and I might be terminal? I can't believe I put people thru this! The truth was I did have an incurable disease and I was going to die if I didn't get help. I was supposed to go to my sisters for Christmas that year and I promised myself I wouldn't screw that up! On the night before my 7am flight a friend called me up and said lets go grab a beer I said no man I can't I have to get up early but of course he talked me into it and next thing you know it was 3 am and I was wasted but I was already packed so I set me alarm got my pills ready and laid down big mistake! I woke up at 615 I ran to my roommate's room and woke him up saying we got 30 minutes man! He gave me a lift and somehow I made it but I felt like shit and somehow I had dropped my morning oxy in my haste so now I was hung-over with no pills I could get to before we landed 6 hours later. Well I made it with the help of quite a few drinks and got to my sister's house. I got my pills out of my bag they were mixed in with a bunch of vitamins that's how I always traveled. I started drinking the minute I got there but it wasn't enough so I had to get creative so I started putting white wine in sipee cups and kids cups because my sister had 2 young kids at the time and so I could get away with a lot of those cups sitting around. But I was sick and exhausted both mentally and physically so I pretty much just laid around hoping I didn't run out of pills before my trip home which of course I did. So as soon as I got back home to Las Vegas there on the floor of my bedroom was the oxy I had dropped rushing to get to the airport so of course I crushed it up and snorted it but the effect was less than desirable and I knew I was coming to the end one way or another. About 2 weeks after I got back to Vegas and to work at the border grill in Mandalay bay where I was a waiter something happened that would radically change my whole existence. See I had worked there for about a year and a half and in that time I had gone from someone who was super grateful for the job to a pathetic drug addict and alcoholic who could not even make it thru my shift without going to the bathroom and drinking 2 or 3 airplane bottles a night for my 4 hour shift plus I always would either snort some oxy or cocaine as well just to make sure I didn't get sick. Now plenty of people had noticed my behavior and I would repeatedly hear comments like it really smells like booze around here or what is that smell? So I started putting fabreeze dryer sheets in my back pockets and in my socks so I would smell fabreezy fresh instead of the walking dead. But I also had started shorting my support staff like the bus boys and bartenders on their tip outs because honestly I was barely making enough to buy all the drugs I needed to function and after I had been warned numerous times more than needed I'll still never understand why I thought that taking 3 or 4 bucks off each tip out would make a difference not to mention these were also my friends and it was just a shitty thing to do but then again drug addicts aren't known for their integrity or abundance of nice deeds. So on this particular Friday I walked in and the GM said he needed to talk to me and I knew I was sunk. He started off by saying that he really liked having me work there but he couldn't let me keep working there when I was ripping off my fellow employees. I understood and as tears came to my eyes because I was so done I literally looked him right in the eyes with that look of please help me but no words came out and so instead I apologized for the millionth time and walked away with my head hanging low and feeling like the doors of survival had just clanged shut. I walked to the nearest bar which was only down the hall but was a trick because one of my sponsors was a bartender at a restaurant on the way but luckily he was gone that day even though I told myself if he was I would go ask him for help again and sat myself down put a 20 in the slot machine ordered my usual shot of tuaca and a coors light and sat there for about 30 minutes enough to only lose 3 bucks get 3 drinks and bail out drunk and depressed. Just when I thought it couldn't get any worse I called my pill guy to go cop as much as I could before he found out I lost my job and when I got there things looked kind of weird there was a lot of people over at his house but I was buzzed and in a fog so I walked right in to a DEA sting what an idiot! I was talking with one of the guys on the way in and thought he was just another customer when he sprang it on me put your hands behind your head. He then put cuffs on me and told me to sit on the curb where I started to cry I was actually glad I thought now at least I can go to rehab or something I mean I didn't have any drugs on me luckily but I was drunk. Then 10 minutes later he comes out undoes the cuffs tells me to get the fuck out of there and never come back or I would go to jail. That's it? I mean I was so glad I wasn't getting arrested but I was ready for help and I thought that was it. So I went home to figure out where to get my pills from now on. I had enough for the night so I did what I always did went and bought more booze laid on my bed wrote a suicide note explaining that it was nobody's fault I was just a defective human and I had nothing to live for. I smoked, snorted and drank myself into oblivion that night and passed out on my note. The next day I woke up took a shot of vodka threw up in the bucket next to my bed took another shot threw up again took a 3rd kept in down rolled up my suicide note and snorted my last 80 oxy and then waited in the fetal position for about 5 minutes and 17 seconds to 5 minutes and 34 seconds for the pill to kick in so I could smoke a little weed pull the covers back pick up my pants off the floor and start the day. That's how I lived every day for the last couple months of this run. Then my main pill guy died he was an old man in his 70's and had been selling pills and other stuff since Sinatra he was a nice guy and sold pills to cover his ridiculous gambling habit of over 20g a week sometimes. His name was Larry and he would always tell me Chris why do you come over here? You have got so much potential so much to offer I really hope one day I never hear from you again and that you never but another pill from me and that I'll turn on the TV and see you with your own show or something he always believed in me and I was one of only 2 people he allowed or trusted to take him around town to run errands but when he died all the pills went with him. His roommate stole everything and bailed out of the house luckily for me she liked me so she split what was left with me but then I never saw her again and I was out of luck on copping pills. So my last week using started like this I had over 50 lortabs tabs the blue 40; s I had 10 oxy 80's and some soma's and that was how I was going to detox of course by Friday I had run out and started to get sick and I couldn't find ANYTHING to help me so I decided to just detox. I bought a case of wine, a ½ gallon of vodka, some crystal meth and a ¼ oz of weed and hunkered down. On Sunday my phone just kept buzzing nonstop and at the time I owed some people money that you don't want to owe money to so I just ignored it finally at noon I couldn't take it and I picked up my phone and saw all these texts weren't from these gangsters I owed money to they were texts from friends and family congratulating me that my New Orleans Saints were in the super bowl! I remember looking across the room at my Deuce McAllister jersey in my closet and being so sick I fell 2 feet off my bed and tried to crawl across my room to get my jersey but couldn't make it so I snorted some crystal and since I was out of booze I knew I had to get some I order to function so I put on some gym shorts no shirt no shoes and a black leather trench coat and drove to the gas station 4 blocks from my house. Now there comes appoint in every alcoholics life where humiliation is nothing and this was my moment. I was so sick I went in bought 3 22oz ice house malt liquor cans and a bottle of yellow tail merlot I walked out of the gas station popped a can of beer and in the noon day sun in front of family's and everyone else guzzled it letting it run down my body and creating a puddle on the ground beneath me wtf? How did I become the bum wearing gym shorts a black leather trench coat and guzzling malt liquor in a parking lot not caring about anything. Somehow I made it home I snorted more crystal opened the wine and smoked some weed and got ready to watch the game. I was so upset that I was living in filth and reeking of god knows what on the day my team had finally made it to the super bowl but eventually I numbed myself enough to just lay there. I nodded in and out of consciousness for the next 2 hours at the start of the 4th quarter I realized the saints had a chance to actually win the game so I said this prayer out loud dear God if you let the saints win I will try again to get sober if not then please let me die today. Well 30 minutes later, the saints had made an interception and won the game and were the super bowl champs!! I was beside myself not just because the saints had won but because I had no idea how I was going to keep my promise to god! But then they showed this footage from Hurricane Katrina and I saw all these people whose lives had been ruined and they didn't even do anything wrong and I started to weep and I begged god to have mercy on me to help me get sober. Now it would be great if that was the last day I ever took a drink or used a drug and just got struck sober but that's not how life works or at least for me there still has to be a lot of pain and divine intervention to make this happen! I was however willing to try again so I bought some suboxone to help with the withdrawal I got some weed and beer and wine only no hard stuff! It was apparent after 2 or 3 days that nothing had really changed and that god was not going to strike me down with lighting for breaking the deal. He knew I was trying and that it was going to take a lot to make this happen so I kept trying and praying and every day I would get less and less relief from the drugs which at that time was my ONLY solution on how to deal with life. 2 weeks later god would make the final move for me I had been trying to get clean on my own for almost 2 weeks meaning basically that I would lay in bed sick until I had to take a drink or a pill then I would get up get well restock my supply and go back to bed. I wasn't working or looking for a job most of my friends were oblivious to how bad it had gotten so I just quit answering the phone or going out at all. Then on a Friday I called to get my pills and was informed he was out and nothing was coming in for at least a week! I had no one else to call and no more energy to go out and try and cop on the street so I just laid in bed and waited to die. All weekend I just laid there sick as a dog cursing everyone including god for making me like this. Finally just as I was about to come out of the mandatory 3 day detox he called and said I have 10 roxys a hundred bucks now or I'm selling them to someone else so I crawled out of bed threw up twice got in the car in just shorts and some slip on vans and drove across to north Las Vegas to his motel and picked them up. He said 2 things when he saw me 1 was that's all there is for a while he was getting out of the business cops were on his back and his dealers were raising the prices so it wasn't worth it then he said you look like shit man you should quit while your tolerance is already down I thanked him for his wisdom and then drove off saying to myself me quit? How about you quit you piece of shit! Anyway I got home crushed up 3 of the 10 I bought cracked a fresh icehouse beer and snorted it all in one line. Fifteen minutes later I had a moment of clarity and decided if I didn't get out of Vegas at that exact minute I was going to die very soon so I loaded up my car which was a soft top Toyota with a broken back windshield torn up seats and leaky windows that didn't shut all the way with some clothes, my skateboard, my acoustic guitar and some artwork I managed to have not hawked and I just took off for San Diego.

An Easter Miracle

I snorted 2 more pills before I left town so I had 5 left pretty much just enough for the night and 2 for the morning so I knew I had about 24 hours until I was completely fucked. I was so bad I actually stopped off in baker and had a couple of beers to make it to San Bernardino where I bought a 6 pack to get me thru the rest of the trip then about 10 pm I pulled into San Diego to my friend Rich's house he was and still is my angel and one of my best friends. Hollywood he said as he opened up the door giving me a big hug how you doing man? I just looked at him and said screw Vegas man I had to get out of there can I use your bathroom? I quickly snorted my 2 nighttime pills then went out to my car grabbed my stuff chugged a beer had a smoke and walked in laid down on his couch muttered a thanks brother you're a life saver and just passed out from exhaustion I didn't know what was next but I knew I had 3 pills for the morning and my best friend and his wife were going to keep me safe and help me get well. Now as much as I'd like to say that this was the end of my torturous journey and that I woke up the next morning filled with inspiration and a solution to my drinking it was not time yet. I mean I tried I really did but I got into a pattern of waking up getting ready going out to look for work but I would need a few drinks for that to happen and one of the things I have learned since getting sober is that I have a 3 fold disease the 1st is a mental obsession the 2nd is a physical allergy the 3rd is a spiritual malady or defect which basically just means that when I not drinking I'm thinking about drinking and when I start to drink everything else disappears and all I care about is drinking more. So that's what happened I would drink 2 sparks in the car every morning to get me inspired but then that would spark my alcoholism and all I wanted was to keep drinking and definitely not look for a job even though I desperately needed one. So instead I would go to a bar by my friend's house in pacific beach called longboards where they had happy hour from 1-3 and would drink a couple of pints and pass out my resumes to people sitting at the bar with me so it felt like I was doing enough not to feel bad about lying to my friend about looking for work but I knew I was treading on thin ice. This lasted a couple of weeks and then I started buying pints of vodka to get me thru the night but I couldn't let anyone see so I hid them in the community laundry room in my friend's apartment complex. I would just pick out a big box of powdered detergent and dig a hole and put my booze in there and mark an x on the outside of the box a genius idea I thought! But finally everything came to a head Rich had a party at his house on the 2nd weekend after I got there and everyone was drinking like crazy I had done my usual hiding my drinking by buying a 6 pack of odouls nonalcoholic beer and then dumping out the odouls and filling it with mickeys malt liquor but I had run out by around 8 so when I saw rich head to the bathroom I went in the kitchen and was in the middle of pouring 2 bud lights into a big blue plastic cup when he walked in and caught me. He said what are you doing and I responded its cool man I got it he said it's cool huh? Then he walked away I knew my goose was cooked but just chugged the beer and walked back outside to the party. Later that night after everyone had left he came into the living room where I was sitting on the couch and he threw something at my head I looked down and it was a 30 day sobriety chip from AA. He said do you remember that? It took a minute then I did and I remembered that he came to my house every day for 30 days a year before I had moved here and gotten me up and out of the house so I didn't take a drink and I had thanked him for saving my life and gave him that chip. He goes for the last year I kept my token next to my bed and thanked god that he let you live and this is how you repay me and he walked away. I was fucking devastated I had finally let every single person in my life down I had been so selfish I had destroyed the last person who was helping me and I felt dead inside. 3 hours later I got up and went to an AA meeting it was 7am and I raised my hand and said I'm Chris and I'm an alcoholic. Afterwards I met a dreadlocked angel named Marvin who had a sober living and said I could move in later in the week if I wanted. I went back to Richs and told him I was leaving and that I was getting sober again he was still mad I could tell and the next 4 days were torture but I moved in to Marvin's sober living I had finally surrendered it was march 9th 2010.

SOBER LIFE

This decision to move into sober living was one of the best decisions I've ever made in my life for this simple reason it is the 1st time I would be held accountable for my drinking. The house was also in Pacific beach 3 blocks from the ocean. Now don't get it wrong this wasn't one of those what I like to call Dr Drew sober living houses this one was disgusting but it beat the streets it was a 3 bedroom 1300 square ft. home with a bedroom for the house manager Marvin and then each room had 2 guys living in it for me that meant 2 twin beds parallel with a walkway of 18 inches between us a TV and a dresser completed the room my roommate was a young and angry 20 something gang kid from northern/central California who just worked out constantly he wasn't bad as people go but living that close to anyone is going to be trying especially with all the supplements and pre work out he guzzled. The house had 2 refrigerators one with a chain and padlock on it for Marvin and the other one for the rest of us and my stuff was always getting stolen which was so aggravating because I had no money and was living on 5 dollars a week in food which usually meant a pack of turkey product from the 99 cent store , mac and cheese cooked and put in 2 different Tupperware containers so I could eat it over 2 days a trick I learned in Hollywood and 2 cans of tuna would round out my meals for the week. They also had this monster 1.99 burrito down the street that was all beans and rice and sometimes I would buy that and split it in 2 for 2 days of food. Times were tough man but I was sober so it didn't matter and I was grateful for everything I had. We got up every morning except Sunday for the 7am meeting called dawn patrol at a place called gods garage just 2 blocks away. That meeting was always packed and it was the 1st time I felt like I could actually not drink for the day. Then after the meeting I would ride this 25 dollar beach cruiser I bought from some guy on the corner. Thinking back I'm pretty sure it was borrowed from someone who wasn't the owner but at the time it was a god send. That bike took me out of my head and gave me freedom to race thru the streets of pacific beach up and down the boardwalk and most important it got me out of the house for an hour while everyone else went back to bed or surfed. Now the house was decorated with a huge bob Marley graffiti painting on the living wall so ironic? There also seemed to be one of everything there was one couch that was trashed and usually had one of the guys who had been kicked out for drinking sleeping on it after they ran out of money and came back vowing to be given just one more chance. I'm all for second or even 10th chances but most of these guys weren't even trying they just would come in mooch all of our smokes steal our food and then disappear again but since our front door didn't lock there wasn't much we could do about it. So we had 1 fridge, 1 couch and 1 bathroom for 9 guys!! Boy that was the worst! WE all had chores to do so at least it was usually pretty clean but still there was never anytime you could actually relax and take a dump or a shower without some guy pounding on the door. So as I was saying I would get up every morning except Sunday at 645 go to my 7am meeting then go for my bike ride come home and go to this run down gym that was connected to our house the gym constituted of rusted out free weights and a broken down universal stand-alone machine but it was better than nothing and free with our rent. It was run by the owner Fred who was somehow the owner of some decent property but had let it go to crap and would let homeless people sleep in the gym for random amounts of money so sometimes you'd be doing your work out and some guy would just be sleeping in the shower or on the floor but like I said it was included in our rent and I had been living on the Hollywood Blvd. homeless scene for a while so it was like Beverly hills compared to my last adventure. After the gym I would finally get my shower time then I would eat my lunch go to the beach and do my step work or go to the library and look for a job then I would go to the 230pm meeting at the north shores alano club 4 blocks down the street from my house. Then spend the rest of my day walking around and staying sober till 6pm when the next meeting was. Some days my sponsor would come get me and we would go to a different meeting or go to dinner. Now when I say I was struggling to stay sober this is what I mean one day I was walking to the morning meeting at 655 and I saw a wine bottle laying on the ground it was a chardonnay bottle with maybe 2 sips left in it. It was laying in someone's yard and I actually without thinking went to reach for it when I had my hand on it someone called my name out Chris! I turned around and it was my friend Ethen coming to join me thank god because I might just have picked that up and chugged it I was that powerless over alcohol even 2 weeks in. I also got a phone call about this time from my friend Rich from

Baltimore we used to work together party together and he was like family to me. The phone call went like this him... Hollywood what's up brother guess what? Me what? I'm getting married brother and I want you to be my best man. I said I don't know man I mean congrats and all but I'm trying to get sober again brother cause if I don't I'm going to die. He goes don't worry brother it's not for a year by then you will be fine and you can get fucked up with me just like old times brother!! He just didn't get it and I understand he wasn't an alcoholic so to him not drinking was just how he was all the time. I said send me the info and I'll see what I can do brother? So after looking for any job I could find for about 2 weeks I finally landed a sales job for one of those independent marketing companies. You know the ones that sell direct TV at Best Buy or home improvements at home depot? It was a commission job and even though I hated it everything is for a reason and that job kept me sober and got me to quit smoking cigarettes as well.

So this is how I got sober I moved into that sober living to hold me accountable and to go thru situations that normally who have had me drink. Then I got this sales job but I would have taken any job offered to me at that point. My daily routine looked like this I got up at 645am and went to an AA meeting came home from that at 8 or 815 got in the shower and left the house by 845 then drove to mission valley from pacific beach about a 20-30 minute drive at that time of the day to the office where we would practice sales pitches and get ourselves ready for success then I would drive from mission valley to Chula Vista about a 30 to 45 minute drive to a best buy where I worked from 12 to 9pm then I would drive back to the office turn in my paperwork and get home around 1030-11 then I would go for a walk on the beach for about an hour listening to Social Distortion, Bullet for my Valentine or some other punk rock bands to clear my head I would also look to the stars and pray to a God I still didn't understand yet but I knew had started to watch over me. Then I would go home read some of the big book of Alcoholics Anonymous and finally go to sleep around 1230am I did this 6 days a week for about 4 months and it might sound crazy to you but that was exactly what I needed to stay out of my head and stay sober. This is also when I had what I would learn was called a God shot and that means when god did something for me that I could not have done myself. One day on my way to work I was driving down the highway and it was summer so it was like 85 degrees I had no AC so the windows were down blowing hot air on me I had 2 dollars to my name I was almost out of gas I was sweating like a pig and I went to grab my last cigarette which had been in a pack in my pocket when I opened the pack I discovered that I had broken it! Oh my God I lost it and for about 2 minutes I let every cuss word fly from my mouth I was cursing everything in my life and then one of my favorite songs and anthems came on the radio which was ac/dc's highway to hell and all of a sudden I felt a peace come over me and I realized what I had for once and not what I didn't have I had a place to live enough gas to get to work and home I had a job and I was getting paid the next day I had a sack lunch next to me and I had almost 4 months of sobriety I had some new friends and this feeling of gratitude just overwhelmed and I realized I wasn't on that highway to hell anymore and that I was going to be ok and you know what? I had wanted to quit smoking anyway so this was my chance to start because it would be a good 10 hrs. Before I could bum one from someone back home. Then all of a sudden one of my all-time anthems came on the radio Social Distortions when the angels sing which I had never heard on the radio ever before!! I will never forget that day God really let me know he was there for me and I was under his care once again. I also got a sponsor right away I heard him speak at a meeting and he started off his talk by saying when I got sober the 1st thing I noticed was that my dick shrank I thought that was hilarious!! I also seem to be the only one laughing so I knew he was the right one because I used to laugh and was always the funny one but drugs and alcohol had taken all the laughs and fun out of my life and I wasn't laughing about anything when I got to AA.

Stepping it up!

I was a pissed off scared little kid trapped in a 40 year olds body in fact I used to get angry at people who would laugh during the meetings because I was in so much pain I thought they were making fun of me. So when I asked Peter to be my sponsor it was a big deal to me. I had Wednesdays off so we would meet in the late afternoon go to a meeting and then work on my steps. Now working the steps was extremely difficult for me because I did not want to get honest or rather I did not know how to get honest I had been lying to myself and everyone around me for so long I really didn't know the truth from my delusions but Peter was very patient. I remember one of the very 1st hurdles we overcame was step 2 see step 1 was a no brainer for me was I powerless over alcohol? Of course I mean look at my life? And was my life unmanageable? Once again obviously I was one of what the big book talks about a self will run riot! Usually I didn't think so but if you looked at my life and all I had drank and drug away it was impossible not to come to the conclusion that both of these statements fit me to a T. Now Step 2 was did I believe that a power greater than me could restore me to sanity? I said no. He said well then we have a problem I said yea what that is? He explained that we couldn't move forward until I did so I told him it's not that I don't believe he can restore me to sanity it's that I have no idea what sanity is peter? I moved out of my parent's house at 15 moved to Hollywood and never looked back and I have no idea what sanity even is. Is aid I even have a bumper sticker on my car that says I don't suffer from insanity I enjoy every minute of it! He went on to explain 2 things that would change my life the 1st was the sanity they were talking about was the fact that when I was sober for any amount of time I would make this decision that I could pick up a drink or a drug and tell myself that this time the outcome would be different than what had happened before. The 2nd thing he said I'll never forget he said well even if you're not sure do you believe that I believe that he can restore you to sanity? I looked him in the eye and said you would do that for me? See it had been a long time since someone wanted to take a chance on me and I barely knew him so I said yes! We moved on to step 3 and once again I hit a road block step 3 says turn your will and your life over to the care of god as you understand him. Well since I still didn't understand him how could I do this? Peter told me to pick something that was bigger than me and that I believed could keep me sober and once again I had tried everything and nothing had worked so over the next month I chose mike ness from social distortion, I chose Pam Anderson, I tried the ocean, they worked but I didn't feel a 100% behind them so I started with Good Orderly Direction meaning as long as I didn't drink or hurt anyone it was a good day. Then I started having these feelings that were in my heart and would happen every time I listened to Stevie Ray Vaughn and like me he was an addict he was also dead which made me think of him more like an angel and every time I listened to his music I would feel a calmness about me. Eventually I would come to believe in God again and I would use him I also changed my acronym from Good Orderly Direction to the saying I use today which is Gratitude or Death.

Now one of the biggest turning points in my sobriety came at about 6 months in. I had been working, going to meetings working my steps and had completed them things were better than ever. About 2 months earlier my friend Sarah who I sat next to every morning at my meetings told me that social Distortion was coming to town and we should go! Well I already thought she was awesome and had a crush on her so combine that with Social Distortion being my favorite band it was a no brainer. So fast forward 2 months later and it's the day of the show about 4pm and I get a text from her saying she never bought her ticket and it was sold out. I knew it would sell out and couldn't believe she had not gotten a ticket or that I had not bought 2 tickets! So being a knight in shining armor type I said I would go down early and see if I could scalp a ticket. Now very few bands have no scalpers 7 social D is one of them NOBODY ever sells their ticket after buying them. But I went anyway I was dressed to the nines in my custom made black and red pinstripe zoot suit and felt like a million bucks on the way down to the show it started to rain. I was like really God rain tonight right now?!! Anyway I got downtown to the House of Blues and nobody was selling tickets but I walked around getting soaked hoping for the best. Then I got another text saying she couldn't get any money out of the ATM and she was gonna bail. I was livid mostly because I had really wanted to go with her but also now because I was by myself and had no support to stay sober. But I put it aside and walked in instantly I felt out of place here I was dressed perfect for Social D and it seemed to me everyone else had just come from the beach and they all had 2 things I didn't a drink and a date. But I decided I would stay strong and just do my best. I made it thru the 1st band but I could feel the angst growing min me why would she do this why am I alone why can't I drink it's been 6 months I bet id be ok? All the toxic thoughts flowing thru my head and about halfway thru the 2nd band I lost it and ran upstairs. I took a minute composed myself and did something I had never done I said God please help me and let me be a light to help someone at this show. I felt better and went back downstairs just as the second band was finishing. As I was standing there I saw about 15 feet behind me someone's dad I could tell because he had on dad clothes a brown leather jacket and blue jeans and was with it looked like his daughter. He kept staring at me and finally he came up to me and asked if I knew the band? I said yes been my favorite for 20 years then he asked if I knew the lead singer Mike once again I said yes but that I didn't know them well enough to get him backstage. Then he asked if I knew that mike Ness was a recovering heroin addict to which I replied yes I know that too. He said I thought you might with the way you are sharply dressed I thought you might be a musician yourself. He said my name is Jim and this is my daughter Vanessa I said hi Jim my name is Chris Then he said something I will never forget and to this day brings tears to my eyes he said I don't know why I'm telling you this but about a month ago my son nick died of a heroin overdose. He had these 2 tickets on the refrigerator and I came down here tonight to see if there was something mike would have said they I could have told my son before he died. He always looked up to Mike and said every time he got clean that mike was one of his hero's in sobriety. I was floored I said Jim do you have a minute he said yes so we sat down and I told him my story about how I left home at 15 that I had been a heroin addict for 20 years and how I didn't have a relationship with my father at all and that I had just about relapsed but had prayed for god to send me someone to talk to you and it was him. We watched the band together that night and became great friends after that in fact to this day I still call him Jimdad and love him with all my heart so I know everything is for a reason but that was definitely my 2nd god shot. Now also at this time the folks at best buy had been really noticing my work ethic and they offered me a job at best buy I couldn't believe it would pay twice what I had been making and the hours would be 40 instead on 60 plus and I would get 2 days off. Also around this time my sponsor had decided to move to Denver so I would have no sponsor. I was on step 8 the amends step and I knew if I didn't finish my steps this time I would surely relapse again. So I had heard a guy share at a meeting I went to quite often and after a meeting one day I asked him to be my sponsor and he said yes now 6 years later he is my 17th and I hope final sponsor he has been there for me thru it all but I don't want to get ahead of the story. Then at 8 months sober a guy I knew came up and said he was looking for a roommate he lived down the street from me but I would be out of sober living and back in a regular house with my own room! I couldn't wait there was no love lost when I moved out I only had my clothes so it took me an hour. Cass St Sober Living had been an experience and I have to say it definitely kept me sober and taught me many things about myself and other people and now I always tell my sponsee's if you can stay sober in sober living you can stay sober anywhere! So now that I had a real room of my own and a good job, I was getting back in shape and had actually joined a great gym in pacific beach called shock fitness it was right on the beach and everyone there was really cool and down to earth Chris the manager turned into a great friend and was actually the brother of one of my close friends Jennifer who I had known since I was 18 and working at Jakes Famous Crawfish in Portland such a small world. Anyway after spending years and months stuck in my room a slave to drugs and alcohol just being able to feel the warm California sun on my face and have someone who was glad to see me was a great way to start my day! This is also where my I started one of my community projects I titled Sexy Saturday Smiles. How it started was that every Saturday morning when I would go to the gym I would pass by the farmers market and see these beautiful flowers. Now I have always been a flower guy but these flowers here were amazing and so cheap. Now since I didn't have a girlfriend at the time I decided what I would do is buy the flowers and then donate them to the gym and when people walked in they were always there to make people smile. Chris agreed and so I set it up and did it every week for almost a year before I moved to another town up in north county San Diego. So I was going to meetings 7 days a week, working 5 days a week and working out 6 days a week and I was done with my steps and starting to see the promises come true. But of course as soon as things become comfortable in my life something has to change! Now before I get to that I must tell you as much as I enjoyed going to AA meetings my favorite meeting was on a Sunday night also in Pacific beach at Gods Garage and it was called H.A. which stood for Heroin Anonymous which was pivotal in my recovery. See for so many years I had gone to AA 7 it had helped but I wasn't able to fully share my story because heroin wasn't accepted by AA which is something I understand as a ground rule because AA was designed for alcoholics not drug addicts and there is NA which is more for drug addicts but NA also has a different book and way of thinking that isn't based on the same 12 steps as AA which is what worked for me so the combination of the ability to share about my struggles of opiate use with the 12 steps had finally gotten me sober. Now I had never heard of HA until 2010 and if you're reading this and have never heard of it either don't worry it is becoming more popular and I am doing my best to bring its message to the world. I also have to thank a friend of mine Wayne H who is the one who heard I was a heroin addict and invited me to my 1st HA meeting. Unfortunately Wayne died of a heroin OD a couple years ago after 7 or 8 years clean I understand his pain but will never understand his leaving us RIP my brother. Now in a perfect world we wouldn't need a separation between AA, NA , HA , CA or OA but as advanced as we have become as a society when it comes to alcohol and addiction we still live in the dark ages it is my hope that one day we can all come together and realize addiction is addiction and we are all addicted to something and the 12 steps and program designed by Bill Wilson and.Dr. Bob works for it all but until that day let's just all agree to disagree on what gets us there but agree to what saves us and gives us hope and a solution God and another person understanding what we have gone thru to get there. Now back to my story so as my 1st Christmas was approaching and I had 9 months sober I decided to do something to give back so I came up with Chris "Hollywood's" homeless Christmas cookie give away this decision would eventually start my Buns N Roses Baking company concept years later but at the time I just wanted to stay sober. I made about 50 Christmas cookies and bagged them up in little zip lock bags and put a 211 card in each of them a service that helps homeless people. On Christmas eve when the streets were mostly vacated by everyone celebrating the holiday inside I went to the places the homeless stayed the library's and alleyways I knew all too well and met and passed out over 25 bags of cookies and a story of hope to all I came into contact with. The women thanked me but every guy asked the same question these cookies got any weed in them? I would reply did you even hear my story? I'm trying to stay sober man them cookies don't even have vanilla in them!! You know what? I stayed sober thru that Christmas and realized that by my giving I had received a far better gift then I had ever bought myself the feeling of helping someone get thru a tough night but also that having a cookie is sometimes the best way to stay grateful. So at about 10 months sober I was asked by best buy to go to Las Vegas for CES the biggest electronics trade show of the year. I was excited that I was considered to be asked but scared as heck to go back to Vegas and stay sober. But after talking to my sponsor and some other people it was decided it would be a great opportunity so I went. All I can say about this trip was that God was with me the entire way and it was one of the best growing experiences in my sobriety. It started off with my friend Josh picking me up we were going to drive this was on a Sunday. Now Josh and I were work friends good ones at that but we hadn't hung out outside of work yet. So not even an hour into the ride I got a call from a friend in AA and so I answered it and it was a good thing I did because my friend was having a terrible day and was thinking about drinking so I kept her on the phone for about 30 minutes until she was ok when I hung up I looked at Josh because this was something that most people wouldn't know how to handle I mean a guy you barely know talking someone out of drinking for 30 minutes? I'll never forget this he just looked at me with this huge smile and said that was awesome!! I'm so glad you helped her!! Ever since then Josh and I have been more like brothers that friends we don't see each other that much but you know those friends that are like family? Well that is him and he really helped me and supported me thru this trip but I'm getting ahead of the story. So we made it to Vegas and all was good. We actually had another coworker and friend from Best Buy David who had a time share and he let us stay there so we had a killer 2 bedroom bath and a kitchen so it was an apartment which was great for me because I didn't want to stay in a hotel on the strip with all the booze and gambling. So I wake up Monday morning and in the middle of my prayers my friend Lindsey texted me her brother had just died of an overdose and because I was sober I could help her thru that and remind me of what could happen to me if I screwed up in Vegas. The trip was like that from beginning to end the next day a friend texted me they were getting a divorce and then Wednesday morning another friend texted me of another overdose so I was reminded of the disease every morning. Now I had not been able to get to an AA meeting at this point and was getting a bit jumpy. So finally on Friday we had completed most of our work and I decided to duck out early to go to a meeting. I looked at the schedule and saw one at three pm. The bus went from the convention center right there. So Josh agreed to pick me up at 430 and off I went. Well of course the whole thing was wrong and 3 busses later and a 10 min walk I finally arrived. It was a different meeting then the one I wanted and only 4 people showed up but it was enough for me to share and actually bring the solution to some people that were struggling way more than me. I got done and was waiting for Josh, he was running late at this point& I was hungry and tired it was literally 3 hours since I had started this adventure and I just wanted to go eat. Josh still hadn't shown up almost an hour later and I was not happy when all of a sudden another God shot happened a friend of mine Barbara from Las Vegas came walking thru the door!! Now Barbara was like my favorite aunt in AA and when I had tried to get sober years before in Vegas she would always save me a seat and always listen to me and really get me back on my feet with her constant positive attitude. I screamed Barb! She saw me and came running over and gave me the biggest hug and said oh honey what happened to you I haven't seen you for years? I explained I had moved to San Diego and actually gotten sober and that I was there for work and normally would have already been gone from the AA club but my friend was running late and then she said the following. Chris I have lived in Las Vegas for 25 years been sober for a lot of those and have never come to this meeting before ever but my friend called me about 45 minutes ago and asked me to come with her tonight to this meeting and not only that but tomorrow morning I am moving to Modesto! So I would have never seen you again or known what happened to you. God put us here together for a reason and I just hugged her and said so true. No joke Josh showed up 5 minutes later if you don't believe in some kind of a god after hearing that story I'm not sure you ever will. I had accomplished something I had never accomplished before in my life staying clean and sober for a whole week in Las Vegas! Other cool highlights were that I actually got to spend time with Paula as she was there for work too and after all that we had been thru I loved showing her that I had gotten my shit together and was clean and sober and healthy, I also got to ride in a limo like a big shot! Now you would think that all that was enough but God saved the best for last. See when I had left Las Vegas and went to San Diego I had only left with the stuff that would fit in my car because I thought I would come back and deal with stuff but after getting sober I couldn't risk coming back so I had left all my stuff in my old room. About 3 months after moving to San Diego my roommate texted he was moving and I needed to get my stuff out so I called my friend Lee and being one of my best friends and coolest people in the world he actually went over and moved all my stuff by himself and had kept it for me in storage and now I was able to come back to Vegas and pick it up and see him and more importantly thank him because that was and has been one of the most amazing things anyone has ever done for me still to this day. We are also like family and have been thru a lot together and as I write this both of us have amazing lives and I am so grateful he is a huge part of mine a true friend!

Well after that trip things settled down and before you knew it I had a year of sobriety on march 9th 2011 the 1st year completely sober since I had been 15 years old I was now 41. That one year token was one of the biggest accomplishments I had ever accomplished.

Deuces are Wild

That token would get me thru many rough patches over the next year. So things were going really great and a week later I celebrated my 41st Birth Day by eating the hottest curry it was called phall curry at a restaurant called world curry in pacific beach and got my name up on the wall! Now even though I had a year this doesn't mean I was cured from my addictions I still would get urges and think about taking a drink every so often but luckily the thought would pass before I acted on it and I can tell you that the combination of morning prayer, going to meetings, talking with my sponsor and working with others was working add on exercise and eating pretty healthy and I was not only staying sober but also growing as a man it was slow but steady and for that I was grateful. So towards the end of April it was time for my next big challenge do you remember my friend Rich had called me to be his best man about a year before? Well it was now time for the wedding except instead of having it in Baltimore which was the original plan which I was cool with because then I could have stayed with my sister and not been tempted into any shenanigans. But instead they had made it a destination wedding in Jamaica Mon! Now since Rich is one of my all-time best friends I really didn't want to let him down but Jamaica was a stretch for me even at 1 plus years of sobriety. But my program was strong and after talking with my sponsor I decided to go for it. I love to travel so the whole drinking on a plane because I'm nervous doesn't apply to me I didn't need a drink to travel or anything else. So I got to Jamaica and saw a lot of my old friends from Virginia and the Chophouse where we had worked including my amazing friend Blythe who is pretty much an angel and if you know her you would say maybe even a saint when it comes to friendship and loving her tribe no matter what! She is also a nurse so that should tell you all you need to know. Once I saw her I knew it was going to be ok and I was glad I went. Now if you've never been to Jamaica let me describe it to you it's like a 3rd world country pretty much with poverty running rampant and the resorts are all behind huge gates so it was a real eye opener for me to see people in huts and no utilities living within a mile or 2 of a huge sprawling resort where they probably threw away more food a day then some towns consumed in a month. That being said there is also a pride and love of mankind there that was reminiscent of New Orleans to me everyone would say hi and for those of the lucky ones that worked in the resorts there were never any complaints about anything they were always positive and happy. Even though I had made it I still felt like I needed a meeting and so I was stoked when the concierge pulled up a chair next to me at a lunch and we started talking about his life and how he got the job etc. he also said that most of his family lived in complete poverty and had a lot of drug and alcohol problems I told him some of my story and we became fast friends. Then I decided after I had looked up AA and could not figure out any of the scheduled meetings or how far they were from the resort we were in I asked him hey man you know of any AA meetings? He said what's AA mon? I said it's a place where people who used to drink too much go to talk about how they don't drink anymore and support each other in not drinking. He goes let me get this straight mon it's a place where people who used to drink too much go to talk about not drinking and that keeps them from drinking? I said yes! He goes sounds like y'all need a drink mon and we both laughed. He looked it up for me and it turns out the only meeting was 3 hours away in Kingston on Tuesday and Thursday nights and it was Friday and I was leaving on Monday so that shot that to hell. I wasn't in a panic but I wasn't happy either now also around this time I was texting this woman I had met on Facebook her name was Ms. Frankie and from her picture she was a cute little tattooed punk rocker and she had told me she was a recovering heroin addict as well so of course I thought we were perfect for each other but instead this woman would rip my heart out again and again and eventually I would find out she had used her friends picture to be friends with me and she was on mental illness meds and on this particular day she really messed with my head. I had had a great day with my friend Nicole we had gone cliff diving and I had gotten this cool bracelet from a local. He had handmade it like a friendship bracelet with all the colors of the Jamaican flag and he explained to me like this red is for the blood yellow is for the sun green is for the grass and black is for the people I thought it was bad ass! But when I got back to the hotel I started getting these texts from Ms. Frankie that she was having panic attacks and couldn't breathe and then she was going to the hospital and then she was like I'm in the ambulance it's really serious and then silence. I was freaking out for like 2 hours crying because I thought maybe she had died or that something bad had happened finally after 3 hours I get a text from her brother supposedly saying that she had been intubated and had died on the table but they brought her back and that she was going to be in the hospital for a couple of days but he would text me updates. The time change was about 6 hours I think so it was already 1 am by the time I got this message so I went to bed super upset. Then I got a call at 6 am my time which would have been midnight her time from her and her voice was fine and she was like I hope you're having fun and I was like this is bullshit if you had been intubated you could not talk without a little rasp at least I mean I had been an EMT so I knew about intubation she freaked out and said I was probably cheating on her already and all this stuff I was livid and at the time I wanted to call her out on the BS but I just let it go and I realized she was very sick and that God had once again done for me what I could not do for myself because all this time I spent worrying about her I was not even thinking about drinking myself and after talking to her I remembered all the BS I used to tell people so I could drink and use. That and my 1 year token in my pocket and my prayers to God kept me sober w that whole time. I even had some guy pretend to shake my hand and put a bag of weed in it a common practice on the beaches of Jamaica for tourists to buy weed from the locals I threw it back at him and walked on so proud of myself. It was a great feeling to be there for Rich and Emily his wife and be the positive person I am sober and not the crazy maniac I had been when they had all seen me before I even gave one of the best speeches of my life that night straight from the heart. I had a great time I played on the waterslides, sang ac/dc karaoke, swam in the ocean , went snorkeling , danced and even got my hair braided into dreads all things I would have never done if I was drinking well except the dreads! I was starting to see that being sober was not that bad after all. In fact being Sober was allowing me to start living, laughing and dreaming all over again. So after I got back from Jamaica a new series of challenges and growth presented me once again God really has a sense of humor when it comes to my life. So I had been living in a condo owned by my friends parents there were 3 of us and it was great everybody very respectful to each other and no drama. Well the parents wanted to rent it out for the summer because it's right by the beach and they needed the money so they let us know and gave us a 30 day notice. There's a thing that most alcoholics are familiar with and it's called procrastination and I consider myself a leader in this field even though I pretend to disguise it. I'm much more productive when my back is against the wall is the lie I tell myself the truth is I like the easier softer way also typical of alcoholics and addicts. So it was the 1st of June when they gave us notice to be out by the 1st of July so guess when I started looking for a place? Yep you guessed it on June 25th. I was thinking that it would only take a week to find a place and more important that I could capitalize on the college students who had just left town and needed to find someone fast to rent their rooms so maybe I could get a deal! Well my week broke down like this. On Tuesday my car blew a rod for those of you who don't know what that means it means that I had an old car that required a lot of oil and I had not put enough in it and even had a quart on my front seat when while I was driving to a meeting one night it blew up on the I-5. The triple AAA guy was very nice in explaining to me what had happened without making me look like a total idiot but we both knew it was a rookie mistake on my part. I spent Wednesday and Thursday looking for a place those were my days off so I was riding my bike around the neighborhood but still had no luck. Friday came and I got an email saying everything had to be out by Saturday for the carpet cleaners to come in everybody else had moved out already. Normally I work on Fridays at best buy but on this particular Friday while I was out looking for a place on my bike my work called and let me know that my position had been cut with the new budget but that I could still work part time it would just have to be in a different dept. but that I would have the next week off till I could start. So as I sat on a bus bench with my laptop having no place to live and now I was only going to have ½ my pay to afford a new place and I had no car or money to get one. I pulled out a bag of trail mix to snack on because I was really trying to be as healthy as possible I took a bite of some nuts and heard a loud crack. Yep you guessed it I had broken a tooth off on an almond. I just remember saying out loud God what the hell?!!! Nowhere to live, no car to drive, pay cut in half and now a broken tooth with no insurance? What did I do to deserve this?!! But I didn't pick up a drink because once again God had done for me what I couldn't do for myself my problems were so big no amount of alcohol or drugs was going to help me In this situation. So I prayed instead and this might sound weird but I actually got this sense of calm that everything was going to be alright it's like God was saying hey I got you but you're going to have to stay sober for this next plan to work so I did. That night I went to look at a place in La Jolla which was way out of my normal price range but it turns out this guy had rent control and his mom had passed so he had never had a roommate but needed some extra cash so we talked and he ended up renting to me and the kicker was that my room had an ocean view! I had never had that before or since then but that's how I ended up living with Scott he also worked in the restaurant biz and was usually over at his boyfriends house so that meant I got the place to myself most of the time and I had to thank god for that one. Next came a phone call with my sister saying that they were going to help me get a car but an actual new car because they were tired of always having to help me get these beater cars every year. So that week I also became the proud owner of a brand new Nissan versa drove it off the lot with 60 miles on it I had never owned a new car before and it was glorious not to have to worry about it breaking down. That car lasted me over 120k miles in 5 years until a head on collision with a Harley Davidson took her out for good. I'm not done yet it also just so happened that my friend Danny worked at Cass St fishery a restaurant/wholesale fish market and they needed someone to work at the retail market and the best part was that it was only 2 miles from my new place! So within a 2 week period I had an ocean view, new car and new job and I was still sober my relationship with God was becoming stronger by the minute. Also around this time I started a company called Rock An Amazing Life an organization to help at risk teens affected by mostly heroin abuse in the north county San Diego area after a woman came to an HA meeting requesting help for her son. Her name was Trae and we became friends and got to work establishing this company. I started a daily devotional I called Rock an Amazing day or RAAD. I also started writing poetry again and was even published in a couple of sober publications. It was my 1st try at anything like this but it would actually morph into Buns n Roses Baking Co later down the road. Now also at this time I was heavily involved in a program designed by a company called Landmark Education which is a personal development type facility offering lots of programs on building your life into a way better one I like to call it the 12 step program for over achievers or business owners and I really took to it taking as many courses as I could. The things I learned there and more important the people I met radically changed my life and helped make me the man I am today. One of the definitive points in my life also came when I was in their introduction leadership program. We would go to LA once a month for 3 to 4 months and gather with about 200 other introduction leaders for the weekend and on the second weekend of this course they had what they call a vivid share which is where we had 2 minutes to tell our life story and what we had accomplished since starting at Landmark. They divided us up into 20 groups of 10 then each group picked who they thought had the most inspirational story then the winners went from that to a 20 person competition the 6 finalists and then they would share in front of some judges and the whole class of 200 peers well I made it to the finals and these people all had amazing stories I mean the overachiever rate in this course was about 90% so after we all shared our stories we sat down and they called out the runners up and then came time for the winner and they called my name Chris Stewart from San Diego it was exhilarating to say the least because for the 1st time in my life I had been acknowledged for overcoming my addiction and for helping others and that was and still is one of the proudest days of my life my prize was a Mr. Potato Head ! Humility is where it's at! I ended up working with Landmark over the years as a volunteer helping with other courses and I will be forever grateful to all the friends/family I made there and for the impact they still have on my life today.

So my 2nd sober holiday was approaching and I knew that being of service was the key to my success so I volunteered with my friends Sara and Jillian to feed the homeless for thanksgiving and we had an awesome time! At this point my friend Rich and I were back to being great friends and so I was not only asked to be a guest for thanksgiving but I was given the honor of being in charge of dessert. I went all out as I do in everything and I made these pumpkin pie, ice cream stuffed gourds I was so proud of them and they looked awesome!! Then on to Christmas since Scott was at his boyfriend's house I had the place to myself so I invited my friend Jillian over neither of us had any family close and it was her 1st Christmas sober. We had a great time! She was then and continues to be a huge support to me and we did it up right steaks and jumbo shrimp and that was one of the best Christmas's I have ever had just being so grateful not to be wasted and to have a great friend to spend it with one of the many gifts I have received that didn't need to be unwrapped. Before I knew it my 2 year birthday in sobriety had come up and I couldn't believe it I was really active at this point sponsoring people men and women which isn't allows looked upon positively in AA but I work with opiate addicts and I'm not going to tell someone I can't help them because we are different sexes I'm there to help them get sober not to date them not to mention 1 of my rules was to never date anyone in the program I honestly couldn't take having 2 of me around all the time plus relationships in AA are twice as much work as other relationships. All this gossip from other people there is the running everything by each other's sponsor etc. and that was never worth it to me so I have no problem sponsoring women even today but I do always suggest once they get some sobriety that they switch over to a woman for other life challenges that I might not understand. It was also at this time that I had to move again I had been approached by a guy at a meeting to be the sober manager for his sober living. At 1st I was a bit hesitant because I hated sober living but after some prayer and talking it over with some people I changed my point of view because it wasn't about me anymore it was about helping others and that is also what I loved to do so I gave Scott notice and moved out for once under friendly circumstances not because I was being kicked out or because we didn't like each other. If I saw Scott again to this day we would hug it out because we are still friends. Now the whole sober living manager thing was a whole set of new responsibility's I had to be there for medications twice a day plus my job and my other personal things so it's a full time commitment. I was given my own room and free rent which was huge for me saving me over 700 a month. Now there are so many personalities in sober living it is usually impossible for everyone to get along and while I was the boss I tried to give the guys enough rope to hang themselves without me doing it so they could learn some lessons and still be in a safe environment. This is also where Buns n Roses got its start in a broken down oven where the temperature gauge was broken and it only had one rack but still I created a lot of cupcakes and cakes for sober people at this house. Eventually we all got into a routine and for a couple of months it was a godsend. There is a lot of personality in a place like this I mean 8 guys with very little sober time there was a lot of meltdowns but also a lot of growth as well I would have kept doing it but I gave one of the guys the benefit of a doubt after a medication screw up. What had happened was that he had gotten a new script and the house rule was that you had to give it to me right away so I could monitor and dole out the meds but he had kept it for 5 days before telling me and it was a heavy sedative for his condition not just some penicillin or something. Well after he told me and gave it to me I told him that I wouldn't say anything to anyone because I didn't want him kicked out he was a good kid he had just made a mistake and so I gave him a break just like I had been given. The problem was that it was a house rule and not a Chris rule and of course the owners of the house found out and called me out on it and I told them what had happened and a rule is a rule so they gave me walking papers. Two things I learned from that A. my rules don't apply to every situation and that it's not up to me to decide someone else's path. I take full responsibility for that and at the time I was pissed but of course God had another plan for me and within a couple of days I would be in an even better situation. I had a friend Peter who ran another sober living up in Encinitas and he needed a sober manager for his place and the consensus around town at the time was that I was a great choice. Now the only problem was that I didn't want to move up north 15 or so miles from where I was at. So he suggested that I come up and look at the place and that's all it took I mean this place was like the Taj Mahal of sober living's it was a beautiful home with a 100k kitchen complete with a full Viking appliance kitchen and a rose garden so my 2 favorite things were in full abundance. So I readily agreed and I'm so glad I did because this is where Buns n Roses really took off I mean to cook with Viking appliances is the dream of pretty much every baker and even though I had a nice 30 minute commute to the fish market it wasn't that bad I mean I grew up in LA so anytime you had to drive under an hour we called it your neighborhood so 30 was nothing. But this place was awesome! I didn't have to dole out any meds I just had to help the guys out with whatever they needed make sure they went to meetings and for a while I actually sponsored most of the guys living there so it was like one big happy family. Everything was going great so I decided to take a trip up i-5 in the summer to go see all my friends up in Portland for the Jake the alligator man festival in Long Beach Washington it is a cool hot rod , rock n roll and burlesque festival the 1st weekend in august. Now since I had my new car and money I decided to road trip instead of fly I love being on the road and this would give me a chance to see a lot of my friends and family who had not yet seen me sober. It was 1800 miles one way and even though I was in great shape mentally, physically and spiritually I still lived like a homeless junkie sometimes for instance the whole way there instead of eating in restaurants and staying in hotels I mean I had the money. Instead I slept in my car and ate at the grocery store still afraid I go broke. Anyway I went to San Francisco and saw my friend Heidi then to Sacramento to a see a girl id never met face to face we were Facebook friends and being the hopeless romantic I am I thought maybe it was fate instead it was awkward and something I don't recommend doing unless your motives come with less expectations than mine! But it was still a good experience that I learned a lot about myself from. I drove like a maniac and arrived in Portland about 18 hours from San Diego and it was great to see my childhood friends and to be sober, I also got to go to voodoo doughnut my favorite donut place in the world. I stayed in Long Beach with my life time friends Mel and Jean. who if you remember from when I was 16 Mel took me to LA and Jean was my 1st adult girlfriend they had hooked up and gotten married and had 2 kids so they moved way out to the burbs but they liked it so more power to them. The weekend went really well and I go to make amends to a lot of my old friends and I made a lot of new ones the festival was off the hook and it was great to be there as the real me to help out wherever I could and not be the drunk junkie I had become the last time most of them saw me. Paula even came down from Seattle so I could meet her 2 amazing boys so it was definitely worth the drive. I headed back and went to southern Oregon to see my relatives and that was very healing for me because I had not seen them since I was in my teens and I had missed them a lot. So all in all it was one of those lifelong trips where very thing had come full circle for me from being born in Portland to moving to LA and playing rock n roll I had traveled the I-5 hundreds of times but never sober since before I was 15 and when I got back to San Diego I was even more focused on sobriety and kick starting my new life in Encinitas. 2 Weeks later something would happen that would change my life and sobriety forever and the story goes like this.

I was on my way home from work at the fishery at about 930 when I realized that I needed some blueberry's to make my lemon on a prayer Sinnabuns for a buns n roses order. At this point I was just getting orders and having to burn the midnight oil to get everything accomplished I knew traders Joes was closed and so my only option was a store called sprouts an awesome little store on the west coast that has fresh produce for really cheap and I knew they were open till ten but I couldn't remember how to get there because I was still new to my city but I made it at 950 and got the look I knew so well from being in the restaurant business for so long we are almost closed buddy hurry it up we want to go home look. So I ran to the produce section and NO BLUEBERRIES! So I made a lap and when I came around the corner there she was this drop dead gorgeous blond covered in tattoos and we looked each other up and down. I turned back around for a final lap around the store still no blueberry's and when I came up to the front she motioned me to her register which had been closed but now was open just for me. She asked did you find everything you were looking for and I said no there's no blueberry's and I'm in a bind she said come with me so she took me to the back and sure enough no blueberry's she then went around the corner and came back with you guessed it blueberry's! So as I was checking out I noticed 2 more things about her 1 her name was Christina and 2 she wore a star ring just like the one I had worn for over 10 years and so I said wow your name is Christina and mine is Chris your covered in tattoo and I'm covered in tattoos and we have the same star ring this is destiny to which she replied yea destined to fail but she was cracking up and smiling at me at the same time. I took it as she felt the same way we both laughed and I thought she's got spunk I like that so I checked out and we said goodnight it was sept 16th 2012 at 958 and I had just found my new muse and love of my life or so I thought. The next day I took her a cinnamon roll to explain what I had been making the night before and I was so nervous I kept fidgeting trying to pay her for a protein bar she just kept smiling and I said umm do you think I could and Before I finished she wrote down her number and said here you go is this what you wanted? Then we both cracked up.

    10 people were waiting in line we kept laughing until my card finally went thru I went home on cloud 9 and called her 30 minutes later when she got off and we talked for an hour. We had a lot in common we both didn't talk to our dads, we both loved music and tattoos but we were different enough that it wasn't an instant connection but still enough to agree to meet

on Saturday when she got off work. So on Saturday night I went to meet her. She was just getting off work now me being me I had already made this into the meeting of the best relationship ever and she was just giving me the after work drink hour to make sure I wasn't some psycho. Now I had never really dated anyone sober before even though I was 40 years old at this point. I had been sober in some other relationships but not 2 years sober ever. So I should have realized I wasn't ready for this when I ordered an O Douls to drink. Nonalcoholic right? Now I was honest with her when she asked why I was drinking nonalcoholic beer I said I don't drink I'm clean and sober which was fine with her since evidently her last relationship was with someone who had issues with drugs and alcohol. But for me it was the start on not being ok with who I was as a man to be dating this beautiful woman. We had a few laughs and it was decided we could hang out again the following week. What that turned into was me and her making out in the parking lot of her work every night after she got off work. Things were going along fine but I knew that she also would ignore me for a day out of every week usually on her day off which was weird to me until I found out she was also dating someone else and when I confronted her she said he was just a friend so I let it go until Halloween. Halloween is my 2nd favorite holiday Christmas being my 1st I'm kind of a cross between Clark Griswold and Freddy Kruger anyway when I tried to make plans for Halloween she said she already had plans. I was upset but once again she promised it was just with some friends and she couldn't get out of it and at this point she was also spending the night we weren't having sex yet just hanging out. Now this was also a difficult spot for me since I lived in a sober living house as the manager I thought the rules didn't apply to me. After Halloween things got different she was distant and I knew something had happened with the other guy but once again I hadn't been in a healthy relationship or sober so I chalked it up to me being over dramatic or controlling so I let it go. During the holidays I was busy with Buns n Roses but also had lost my job at the fishery so I was unemployed and that also made me feel like I couldn't pursue her because I didn't have a lot to offer. But after a Christmas blow up where she cancelled her plans with me last minute I decided no more chances. She kept texting me like everything was ok and so I thought maybe she had come to her senses I had also become friends with her best friend Lisa who would tell me the behind the scenes stuff not details but just that she wasn't sure which guy she wanted to be with. Well there was no way I was going to be 2nd fiddle and after she gave me some crappy excuse for not hanging out on New Year's. It was after that night that we had one of only 3 fights we would ever have about our relationship. So being the great codependent I was. I told her that I loved her and gave her an ultimatum me or him. Looking back I realize anytime you give an ultimatum you have already lost the fight my dad did it to me and I had done it to many others over the years and it never worked out but lust can make a man do crazy things so that's what I did. She said she needed time so I told her take all you want but I am done. After 3 or 4 days she called me and said I was the one I was so happy and never took an inventory of the resentments I had building and just jumped in. Now I will give her this when she has made up her mind she sticks to it and I no longer saw any texts from any guy or her hiding her phone from me for over a year. I had also gotten a job right on the beach at a restaurant and was back making great money. I took 3 years on March 9th 2013 and was on top of the world. The following week I had the one of the best birthdays ever Christina and I went to Yomishiro my favorite restaurant in LA and got a table right at the window overlooking all of Hollywood. Then we went to see one of my favorite bands Volbeat at the house of blues I couldn't have asked for a better day we got home late but the next morning we even had sex for the 1st time 6 months after we had met but I finally felt like we were a couple. but there was the problem with working so much and hanging out with Christina all the time I had quit going to meetings and quit sponsoring most of my guys a lethal combination I had put her above my sobriety and my relationship with my higher power and then came the day when I was asked to try some wine at work. The whole thing took less than 2 minutes and went like this Chris I know you don't drink but can you try this wine the guy who ordered it says its bad and it cost two hundred dollars I don't know what it's supposed to taste like? I thought to myself for a second yea I don't drink so of course I'll help you and I took a drink and the worst thing happened for one the wine was bad but also it didn't make me go crazy or start drinking go to Mexico and buy heroin or anything it had no effect on me at all. I went home to the sober living, talked to Christina and checked on all the guys in the house just like any other day but when I laid my head on the pillow that night the thought occurred to me hey I drank tonight and nothing happened maybe I'm cured? Cunning, baffling and powerful this disease is and it had just won me back to the dark side. Then just a few days later I was offered a glass of champagne and I didn't even hesitate as I took that drink the demon was awakened and I got the same feeling of ease and comfort that alcoholics get when they drink and just like that 3 years went down the drain. Now I still didn't get drunk but I knew that I had crossed the line. Now Christina is in no way an alcoholic in the 2 years we were together I only ever saw her drunk twice both times were with other people not ever when it was just the 2 of us. She did like to drink wine though with dinner every night or after she got off work so I started buy her wine and putting it in my room the only problem was Id pour her a glass then I would drink the rest of the bottle when she wasn't there or before she came over. I also had started drinking at work the restaurant was going out of business and all the employees would just help themselves it was a toxic environment but I was making good money so I didn't care. By the time May and June rolled around we were the it couple and doing everything together I was able to drink a glass or 3 of wine every day and still handle stuff even though I was still the manager of the sober living I had become a real ass hole to the guys though running it like a dictator and they were starting to complain and move out. After shopping one day and running across a wedding ring we both loved I decided it was time to make the move so I took all my savings and bought this beautiful 8k ring. I mean I had a great place to live I was making a fortune at the restaurant I had it made so why not get engaged? I planned a special trip to Solvang a Danish town up by Santa Barbara and planned the perfect day WE started by going to my favorite Cajun restaurant in Santa Barbara called the palace café. Then we headed up to Solvang and checked into the hotel and I had let the hotel know ahead of time my purpose so they upgraded us to a beautiful 2 floor suite. We shopped and went to the local farmers market and I bought her roses and a couple of other cool little gifts then suggested we go back to the room to change for dinner. When we got to the hotel I had her sit on the patio in this little courtyard and I went up to the room to get the champagne and a photo album that I had made of all of our dates and special events we had done. I also needed to drink a couple of mikes hard lemonades to get in the proper spirit. I came down and gave her the album and asked her to be my bride in between tears she said yes and then we had the hotel capture the moment on film! What a glorious day we went up to the room and while she fixed her makeup I drank the champagne and got a good buzz heading to dinner. I was on top of the world and when we got to the restaurant I ordered more champagne explaining to her normally I don't drink but I want to celebrate with you. Non alcoholics don't always know the full story of alcoholism so most will let the person have a drink for special occasions I made sure not to go crazy and just enjoy myself and the dinner was amazing root is the restaurant and I highly recommend it. She looked stunning in her white pants and tight fitting aqua marine sweater a perfect complement to her sparkling green eyes and I was head over heels for her. I had finally achieved a perfect life again. When we got back to San Diego we were like the king and queen but my drinking was getting worse and I couldn't stop. Now I had been a drunk most of my life but when I was sober I had received all these gifts of the program and now I had let them take me back out and I was running scared. I didn't want to lose her, lose my job and lose my place to live even though I wanted us to live together. God has a way of doing for me what I can't do for myself and within a week of our engagement I was informed the house had been sold and we all had to move out. I was devastated not only because I had just spent all my money and had none to move but because now I wouldn't be in a sober living which meant all bets were off on my sobriety and I was sure to get worse. So we started looking for a place to move in together and by I mean her, She was and is very particular about everything she does she eats her banana's from the opposite end of most people, she won't eat avocados if they even have one brown spot on them and she won't live in apartments preferring tiny guest houses which was cool with me because I don't like apartments either. So she found a place in Escondido which is not at all where I wanted to live but happy wife happy life right? So I went and met with the owners of the house because it was my bank roll paying for it. It turns out the house was owned by a pastor and his wife and they were very nice I was also thinking that even though I didn't like the area I was engaged to the most beautiful woman at the time to me and I could use more God in my life so moving in to a guest house of a pastor was perfect for me plus I knew Christina would be safe the times I wasn't at home. So we moved in 2 weeks later lock, stock and barrel. It was her and I and our 3 minkeys or Persian cats Mama Marshmallow, Minkey Jah Bob and of course Panderella our rescue cat. In the beginning everything was great we love to shop so shopping for all new house stuff is always fun we bought a chandelier even but when we got it home it was way too big and we never even hung it. Now the summers in Escondido are brutal there is a desert wind and we had no AC so our house was constantly a sweat box so between that and being drunk all the time I was not very pleasant to be around but we made the best of it. I also realized after moving in that she did not even come close to having the same sexual energy as I did and that was another problem but like I said I was a workaholic and drunk so I didn't make a big deal out of it for fear of getting crap for my drinking. As the summer continued we still had our moments and were still in love but the co- dependency and drinking were making my life such hell that there were nights driving home on the Del Dios highway where I literally just wanted to drive of the road and plummet to my demise. This had nothing to do with her my reason was because I could not stop drinking and when I mean stop I mean like every 3 to 4 hours of every day I had to have a drink it was just like before I had quit 3 ½ years earlier except that I still had a job and my fiancé. Now if you know me you know I love New Orleans I love the food the people the French quarter and Frenchmen street but most of all I love the New Orleans Saints and have for over 30 years all the way back to when they were called the aints. SO I decided for our 1st Halloween together I would take her to the big easy it also happened to be the Vampires Ball that year even cooler! So I worked double shifts for about 3 weeks and saved up enough I even took her to Hollywood to get her costume perfected and we made a plan. Now my plan was to get sober before we went because if you remember New Orleans was also my demise on my honeymoon with Paula and it didn't want that to happen again. I tried to work out more and not drink during the day but within a day or 2 I'd be right back at it and at work I really needed it I told myself I mean all those double shifts how could I expect to keep up my positive attitude without a little lubrication? Let me give you a little bit of my daily drinking pattern so you understand. I would wake up before Christina and either finish off the half bottle of wine I had stashed in our guest room or if she was already at work then I would just drink 2 mikes hard lemonades I would then go to work at 10 am and start with the champagne because I loved champagne and it was my job to set up the restaurant so nobody even noticed I only drank the brunch champagne because we had a ton of it and it was untraceable usually 3 or 4 mimosas later I would work thru lunch then on my break I would go to a liquor store and buy 2 more mikes hard lemonades and 2 airplane bottles of flavored vodka then suit in my car and drink those before my night shift and that's when the real drinking would start I could put down between 4 to 6 double vodka lemonades before the end of my 3-4 hour dinner shift then I would get 2 hard mikes for the 40 minute drive home getting home around 10 and having a half bottle of wine to finish off the night now some days were different than others but that was usual. How I actually drove home every night thru this windy mountain pass road is a miracle and definitely gods work not mine. So it came time for New Orleans and I couldn't wait I had dinner reservations at my favorite restaurant commanders palace. I also knew that my favorite jello shots made by Uncle Johnny at the court of 2 sisters would hit the spot. We got to town and hit the French quarter 1st thing for oysters at Acme I ordered a beer while she went to the bathroom so she wouldn't know and then told her it was a non-alcoholic beer when she returned. We had oysters and beer and were having a great time we ended up calling it a night pretty early because she is like a human cat and always ready for sleep and I knew that to keep up with me she would need it. The next morning while she was getting ready I went to the store and started the daily intake of booze and in new Orleans nobody even looks twice at you when you're holding a drink at 8 am it's kind of like Vegas that way. That afternoon I took her to see Uncle Johnny and have a world famous jello shot once again telling her I would only have one and that is was a special occasion I ended up have a total of 5 that day. We had an amazing day I mean New Orleans on a cool fall day sunny eating po boys at Johnny's po boys in the quarter snacking on zapps chips while watching the mighty Mississippi roll by all the juke joints blasting out blues and being drunk it was like falling in love with everything. That night we dressed to the nines and hit commanders where I had one of the best meals of my life and continued with my champagne she was never really present to all of this I don't know why but she just never seemed to be able to really let go and have fun so I did it for the both of us! The next night for the vampires ball we headed out and met some really cool people who we danced with and drank with all night once again I would sneak beers saying they were non- alcoholic and try not to get caught it was a Saturday and on Sunday we had saints tickets, so I was trying to be good but you know the story so Sunday morning found me trying to guzzle enough booze in the hotel bar before we went to the game trying to get over my hangover luckily it took her hours to get ready so I was able to get a good head start. . The saints ended up winning beating the Buffalo Bills and afterwards we rolled to mothers to continue the festivities. If you're an alcoholic you know there comes that point where you just can't get any drunker but you also can't stop and when we got to mothers I hit the wall. I continued to drink but I could feel my body shutting down and my face turning red from alcohol poisoning. I dismissed it as too much hot sauce but really bro? On Monday we were leaving so once again while she was getting ready I hit the hotel bar and got a giant rum and coke for the ride to the airport and this is where it could have all fallen apart because while I was in the bathroom she took a drink because I told her it was a diet coke and she looked at me and said there is rum in this! I played dumb and said I thought it tasted funny I thought it was just flat she poured it out and let it go but it was another close call for me. When we got home my drinking escalated to the point of where I would say I was going to the gym then go buy 2 hard mikes and 2 small wines bottles usually pinot noir cause I'm fancy drink those in the gym parking lot then drive back home and pour my water bottle over my head just as I walked in to make it look like sweat some are sicker than others and at this point I was very sick. I made it to Dec 21st Christina's birthday before I got fired from my job. I was drunk and angry and a customer said something to me which I replied they were wrong and they asked for the manager he came over to talk to me and said your drunk go home to which I replied no I'm not! Now I don't know about you but every time I say I'm not drunk it makes me drunk and then he said you can't even talk and I knew I was done I left there and headed home filled with shame, regret and remorse I had no savings no job and Christmas was only 4 days away. Luckily when I got home we were going dancing with her best friend Lisa for her birthday so I didn't say anything and the next morning I switched to vodka for breakfast. WE made it thru Christmas and actually spent it with her mom. I told her I had a week off for the holiday I didn't know what else to say. Having a job is the number one thing for her because growing up her mom was very unstable and having a job is security to her. I knew I would find something I always did and I had lost more jobs at this point than anyone I knew. 2 days later I received a phone call that would set my sobriety in motion once again. One of my dearest friends and Ruby's best friend had been trying to get sober on again and off again for years but with no luck and so when Ruby called me at 730am on a Tuesday I knew something must be wrong normally I wouldn't even be up but I had a case of the shakes and didn't want Christina getting upset so I was in the kitchen drinking wine out of a coffee cup. I answered hey what's up? She said Kelly wants to go to rehab but she wants to talk to you 1st because you are sober and she trusts you and I looked into my reflection in the wine of the coffee cup and felt like the world's biggest loser and hypocrite put her on I said. I talked to her for about 10 minutes and gave her the pep talk I had heard so many times myself and I decided I was going to get sober too again now this is where ego really comes in because the only reason I really wanted to get sober wasn't because I had run out of money and free booze at work but because I didn't want Kelly to have more sober time then me! So the next day I went to a meeting I did not stay sober but at least I went. Then I had the following experience that reminds me who is in charge. On Saturday 3 days after talking with Kelley I went to a meeting and was just done at the end of my rope and afterwards I unloaded on a guy from AA he suggested I go to a place called the friendship center in Escondido a residential detox/rehab facility. I had heard of it but I didn't want to go into a residential because then Christina would find out how bad I was but after I got done talking with him I decided it was my last option so I drove over there. I found the intake desk and told the guy my story and begged to be let in and he said this back to me well I think we could help you but we only do intakes Wednesday so just don't drink anymore and come back on Wednesday I looked at him and with tears in my eyes said if I could quit drinking till fucking Wednesday I wouldn't need to come here!! I left as broken as I think I had ever been in my life I went and bought 2 bottles of wine at trader Joes , 4 mikes hard lemonades from 7-11 and went home to get well before Christina got home. The next day was New Year's Eve and Christina was going to be at work till 8. About 730 I realized I was not going to have enough to make it thru the night even with the bottle of champagne I had bought for a new year's toast with Christina so I made a trip to 7-11. I was wasted and tired but I didn't care. I had also been pulled over on a couple different New Year's eves over the years and didn't want to chance it but I had no choice so off I went. As I pulled into the parking lot a guy pulled up right next to me and it happened to be a guy from AA I knew and who had also helped me change a flat tire a couple weeks back on my car when I was drunk and just leaving a meeting. He looked at me and I looked at him and I knew God had sent me an angel I did not have the strength, courage or bullshit to walk past him and buy booze so I just waved and went back home empty handed. Christina got home and we had our champagne toast then we laid down to watch a movie and relax and that's the last thing I remember the next thing I know it was 8pm on new year's day and I had slept over 18 hours which had never happened in my life I knew if I could get back to sleep and make it one more day I would have broken the detox barrier so I prayed to god and he let me fall back asleep and for once Christina's sleeping all day syndrome helped me out. The next day I woke up took a shower and went to the noon meeting and have remained sober ever since my new sobriety date is Jan 1st 2014 but it was no New Year's resolution it was a life saver.

Sobriety Part 2

Keep coming back

I am not going to sit here and tell you that the obsession was removed but I did manage to get back to the gym and start applying for jobs as well and once again god came thru almost immediately I was hired as a manager for a new Vegan fast casual concept called Native foods and they were sending me out of town to Chicago for 2 weeks right away and then Los Angeles for another 6 weeks now for most people that would have killed their sobriety but not for me for me I was so happy because I needed to get sober and couldn't do it in the toxic relationship that Christina and I had going at that time. So on February 8 I took off to Chicago and went from 60 degrees to minus 40 but I had a room of my own a solid 10 hour work training day and then I was able to find meetings at night. One of the weird things about my relationship with Christina was that if we were not together we never talked on the phone only texted we never had a good phone relationship and for that I was glad because I was so filled with resentment at her and myself the one at me was valid the one at her was not because it had been my decision to drink and still to this day she claims she never saw me drink or act drunk in front of her. Anyway I was all too glad to just send a text or 2 to her every day of course we were still engaged so I sent her a Valentine's day card and flowers on valentine's day and at the time I thought once I was sober we would work things out. So Chicago is a great city but the weather was brutal and I couldn't believe it every night while the other managers went out to dinner I would be walking in this minus 20-40 degree temps for sometimes a mile to get to a meeting arriving red faced and frozen to the bone but always welcomed. That's one of the things non alcoholics don't understand about AA and that is no matter where we go in the world there is an AA group that always welcomes us gives us a cup of coffee and asks us to keep coming back and that has saved my ass in many a town or even country over the years. So from Chicago I was sent to Culver City CA and here is where god has a funny sense of humor the restaurant I was training in was just blocks from Ruby and I's house when we were married I mean you want to talk about bringing back some painful memory's wow! But it was also good because I knew all the meetings and even saw some familiar faces. It was tough traveling thru old neighborhoods and having flashbacks of getting drunk or high in the car or remembering stealing things from certain people or business's but it was also close to my favorite donut shop King Donut so I just ate a lot of donuts and it was good to see my friend King again and get my sugar fix. I did come home from LA a couple of times during the 6 weeks I was there but it was different now in fact even on my birthday I spent it with my new friend Ken from Native foods instead of Christina she did meet me in Huntington beach for an afternoon we just ended up sitting in a bar all afternoon with our friend Lisa who came to join us and then went to our favorite Italian restaurant basilicas. When I did get back home I started right back in at the meetings in Escondido and called my sponsor and got back into some step work which was great. I had almost 90 days by the time I got home and was feeling pretty strong. I liked my new job but it was a lot of hours and things at home were different and I'm not the kind of guy that can fake stuff so our relationship had begun to go from wedding bells to hells bells. The weird part was that if you talked to us we would say how in love we were but to me actions speak louder than words and we just didn't have that team mentality in my opinion anymore and a lot of that was my fault because I would specifically tell her we weren't acting like a team but in a not so comforting way. We never fought in fact out of all the relationships I've ever been in Christina and I fought or even argued the least. We would always be friends because we established that early in the relationship but I wanted to be more than just friends in a relationship I wanted passion and unconditional love and I had never really felt that from her or anybody in my liflte would turn out later I was unable to feel it because I couldn't give it but I'm getting ahead of the story again. We l went to weddings and the horse track (dressed to the nines) we went to car shows and watched a lot of movies together but I pretty much became a workaholic and she became a homebody so we only hung out 1 day a week at this point Things were going good though and I was making a stable check I was sober and life moved on. Around September the company started having problems and we had to make some changes so they transferred me to another store almost an hour away and I was livid. I tried to stay grateful but I am not good at masking my feelings and it obviously became apparent because in October the regional manager came to town and for what I thought was going to be a promotion I got fired instead. It was a real shady deal they even paid me my last check from the register in cash. I went home and told Christina or kitty as I had nicknamed her the news and I could see that was the final straw for her and sure enough a month later she started hanging out with friends I had never heard of and then came that day when she said here is the ring back I'm moving out. Even though we had not been happy I didn't want to break up but I didn't really have a reason why we should stay together either and I knew she had been dating other guys all ready and I didn't trust her so it was over. So at my one year of sobriety I had to move again, find another job and I was single right back to the beginning. So I moved her 1st of course because I'm that codependent person still at this point I made sure she had the TV all the housewares and even the bed was hers so I had to go buy a blow up bed to sleep on. Then a day later I got a call from my friend Robert about managing a sober living house for his company and I realized this was my way to make up for the last debacle. My next 3 months were great I really needed to be around sober people at this point in my life and get back on my feet financially I had sold Christina's wedding ring back to the jeweler for a grand and taken a 7k loss on it but at least I had money to move. Now this sober living was a bit different than the last one these kids were also in a very intensive inpatient program so my day was spent dropping them off at the facility then I had a 3 hour break I would pick them back up and then take them to meetings at night but it gave me time to study and attend classes to be an alcohol and drug counselor and more important to do a workbook that would change my life it was called the one way relationship book and it was an intensive book on codependency. I had never known I was so co- dependent and this book literally saved my life and to my friend Father Mike I will be forever grateful for the time you spent getting me thru this work. My whole life I had been relying on other people to make me happy and my expectations of them and me were completely delusion no one could have ever lived up to them . I have never cried like I did going thru this book and looking at my life and also discovering the deep wound I had from abandonment issues stemming from my parents and Ruby, Rachel and now Christina. Unfortunately a lot of the anger I had was still deep inside me and that coupled with fear of my future led me to make some bad choices in the way I treated the guys in sober living and after numerous warnings I was asked to leave so at 44 years old, I found myself single and sleeping on my friend Joes couch with no job but sober and that was when I really learned a lot about myself. I went to some more classes at landmark and my friend Chris there really was supportive and helped me get thru this point in my life. I really found my now current relationship with god during this phase as well because Joe had a recovery bible I had never seen one of these before and basically it's a bible with footnotes in recovery so I could understand how the bible pertained to my recovery. I really started to understand my meditations and prayer on a whole new level. Then things started to really turn for me I got a great job as the GM for a fine dining restaurant in Del Mar and then I got a room in Pacific Beach that had an ocean view from the roof and I started praying and meditating up there every morning. Now this is where things got dicey again because once again I had the gifts of the program a great job, a great place to live I had a couple of sponsee's and was more spirituality fit than ever and the only thing I was missing was a girlfriend so in a moment of weakness I decided to call Christina and tell her how great I was doing it just so happened she was coming to pacific beach that day to get tattooed and so we met up for dinner. Now here is the thing about me and my past relationships I am still friends with all of my ex- girlfriends except for 2 and I mean since I was 15! The other thing is the relationship I had with Christina never got to the hate each other [part we just grew apart and so seeing each other was just natural that the attraction was still there so guess what? Yep you guessed it we started talking and texting everyday again and seeing each other once a week and then the 1st red flag came in because I started sending her letters and stuff in the mail and one particular package came back saying she no longer lived there and to call the postmaster so I called her and she informed me that Christina had moved 3 months earlier and did I want the new address and to send the package there. I was in disbelief so I called her and after really pressing her she told me she had moved in with her ex- boyfriend but that she was already over him and wanted to move out. This is where I should have moved on but instead what does a co -dependent /alcoholic / ego maniac do? Oh I will help you move out and that way we can get back together right? What an idiot I am! So we started seeing each other even though she lived with him still and I bought into all the bullshit she told me about loving me and how she made a mistake and 4 months later she moved out and with the money I gave her moved into a new place. Then I thought we made it official but what I didn't hear or more importantly what I didn't acknowledge her saying was that she didn't want to get into a committed relationship right away but like I said actions speak louder than words so when she kept texting me and calling me every day told me that she loved me and then even gave me one of her precious fur babies so she could live with dad I fell hook line and sinker and even went out and rebought the wedding ring again! That ring would never see her finger. We spent Halloween dressing up together as a cat and mouse team and had Christmas together one of the best I've ever had starting with consummating the relationship Christmas morning. We also spent it with our friend Lisa and it would not only be Lisa's last Christmas on earth but the last one Christina and I would spend together. Also around Halloween I had gotten fired from the restaurant in del mar but luckily I had a great friend Wes who I worked with in Las Vegas years ago and he got me a job right down the road at another restaurant called Mia Francesca which is where I still work today. Now my meditation and prayer were stronger than ever at this point what happened was that the previous summer when Christina and I had gotten back together I had moved to a killer pad in Vista on top of a hill my own house for the 1st time in sobriety and it had what I fondly referred to as my prayer chairs 2 chairs overlooking the valley and when the weather was clear I could see the ocean and in those chairs god and I talked every day for over a year and here Is what I'm talking about. When I moved in I had the GM job and was making a lot of money for me and Buns n Roses was really taking off so I rented this place that costs twice as much as I had been paying but it was my own place I had a huge kitchen a fireplace and a view to kill for. I moved in on a Saturday and the following Monday I went in and got fired. That meant I had no way to pay for this place and I had just spent my 3500 savings to move in. So I started praying like I never had before and the first month I was still short 300 dollars with only 2 days left to pay the rent and guess what? God took care of it the next month the same thing happened and every month for that entire year I would be short on rent 2 or 3 days before it was due and every time god came thru. I also came in second in the San Diego cinnamon roll competition which was no easy feat. I had worked all night come home and started baking at 11pm I finished the 125 cinnamon rolls required at 8 am and drove straight there still in my apron.

Now this is another example of Christina and I's relationship I got home and called her to tell her and she acted like it was no big deal and even though she had the night off she didn't want to hang out but I told myself that it was ok and we would hang out some other time but I was bitterly disappointed. Now on valentine's day weekend I had planned to take her to Hollywood and gotten us tickets to one of my favorite bands Hanoi rocks who never come to America and a hotel room on the morning I was going to pick her up god told me it was time to end this relationship but I thought this can't be right? When I walked thru her door 2 hours later she broke down and said she wanted to break up. I couldn't believe it but I knew in my heart it was supposed to be over but I didn't do it and insisted we go to Hollywood anyway. Needless to say it was a terrible trip and I wish I had just gone by myself. The thing was god had told me specifically what to do and I didn't do it but I also started to listen to my god consciousness for the 1st time in my life and that's when things really started to get me to see the pain I was holding in and trying to get her or anyone to fix when only god could heal this. The next time I went to see her 2 weeks later I was involved in the worst car crash of my life. I was 3 miles from her house and a car swerved in front of me on a country road and when I swerved I hit a Harley going 60 miles an hour nothing I could have done to prevent it and it wasn't my fault but it destroyed my car and his bike and sent him flying. I knew god was saying don't go there but I just couldn't let her go when I finally got to her house she wasn't even worried about me or the accident it was almost like I was inconveniencing her with this information and that day we got in a fight in the middle of the mall and I knew I didn't want her in my life anymore and that would be the last day I saw her for months until we got the news that would bring us back together one last time.

Our friend Lisa actually her best friend and over the years she had also gotten to be very close to me as well. Lisa was actually the reason we still stayed together over the years because she would be the go between when we couldn't say what we wanted to each other. What was weird is that even after we broke up Lisa would texts from both of us for a variety of reasons and they would always come one right after the other at 1st I thought she was just trying to get us back together but then one day she actually showed me her phone and sure enough our messages would come in within a minute or 2 of each other it was very weird but then it made sense later but I'm getting ahead of the story. So back in august of 2015 we got a text from Lisa's friend that she was in the hospital now what made this weird was that Christina and I were not officially together but had actually hung out that day to go visit her mom and we were only 5 minutes from the hospital where she was and that hospital was actually 30 minutes from my house and an hour from Christina's so divine intervention was definitely in place. We got to the hospital and found out she had been in a coma for the last week and was seriously sick with heart disease she was only 47. Over the next couple of weeks we would visit her separately but never together but she got better and moved home. For the next 7 months she was in and out of the hospital and Lisa and I became very close I got her to re new her relationship with god and we began praying together. One day when she was in the hospital and I went to visit god spoke to me and said you pray over this woman. Now I had been praying to myself but I wasn't in my mind a prayer warrior of any kind but I also knew that my intuition needed to be heard so I asked her Lisa can I pray for you? She said yes and for the next 5 minutes a prayer came out of my mouth that had nothing to do with me and had everything to do with god. At the end of that prayer she was weeping and she looked up at me and said that was the nicest thing anyone has ever done for me. The other thing that made this a god thing was that when I held her hand I could see that she was dying and if she didn't change her way of living she would be dead very soon so I started hanging out with her more often giving her encouragement and prayer and she started going to church with me. We would go to church every Sunday and then go to lunch and we really became very close and she had started to get quite a bit better but she still didn't have a lot of energy. I'll never forget every Thursday I would bake a new product for Buns n Roses and I would text her and tell her there was a special treat for her and to come over while I was at work and enjoy it! She would come over and sit on the prayer chairs and get her God on as she called it and I loved seeing her pics of the sunset and her empty plate because I knew that at least for 30 minutes she had a sense of peace. Then on my 46th birthday she actually baked me a birthday cake which no one had done in years. Usually on my birthday it's a big deal to me so I would make my own cake but for years I had been asking people to do it but they all said they same thing I can't bake as good as you Chris and I would say who cares it's the thought that counts and Lisa understood that so she baked me this cake that was a riot it was a cinnamon roll/ring type of cake with some kind of frosting still not sure what kind but I just loved that cake! I only ate 1 piece because it was dry as a bone but it was one of the nicest things anyone had done for me and so we were even. My life was really taking off at this point I was doing a lot of stuff with Buns N Roses and I met a woman named Rochelle and her and her son Ashton started to come over every week and help me bake stuff and it was a lot of fun we baked cupcakes and prayed, rocked out, played pool and became very close friends and it was thru her that I discovered my knack for prayer and hope was really blossoming. We would go on adventures with Ashton and we became like a little family but once again when I was falling in love she was just looking for a friend so I didn't push it and we remain close to this day and I really miss hanging out with her and Ashton baking cupcakes but it's all part of the adventure right?

God Shot Thru the Heart

My next project would take me to places I had never been and had wanted to go for a long time. I had a friend of mine her name was Amy and one day she came to me and told me about this phenomenal leadership program she had just completed and that I should check it out. Well I had seen the change in her over the last year and I wanted in on that so I met up with the guy running the program Brad Ballard and he told me something that I had never heard before and had wanted to hear forever and that was this program doesn't teach you how to program your mind like all the others instead it focuses on your heart and what's really in your heart to drive you so I was in! I decided to do it the only problem was that I didn't have the 1500 to enroll. Story of my life all revved up and nowhere to go and I told my mom about it the following day. Now here is where God comes in my mom said lets pray about it so we did 4 days later my mom calls me and says honey the weirdest thing just happened I got a refund back from my insurance company and I have enough to help you with that leadership program!! So I enrolled and the work I did in that program would completely change my life and the lives of those around me. Now I can't go into detail about the exercises in the program A. because I signed a confidentiality agreement that I wouldn't and B. I don't want to ruin anyone else's experience of it when they take it but I can tell you the following results that I had. The very 1st exercise we had to do had us connect with another human being in a way that I had never connected with anyone before little lone anyone I had never even had a conversation with and with that I was off and running to freedom. The relationships I formed there became family and to this day O would never hesitate one minute to call anyone of the 29 people in this program for anything in my life if you don't have that in your life do this program. Now in order to get to your heart the amount of work you need to do on yourself is almost overwhelming unless what's in your heart is to be of maximum service to others and then it becomes just extremely painful but so worth it. After the 1st weekend I felt like a weight had been lifted from me and not just in a temporary way but in a life changing way and when I talked people could notice. Now just to be candid some of the feedback I got was brutal because if you want to get to your heart you have to break apart the worst enemy most of us have and that is EGO my friends that pesky little creature that ruins our lives and the lives of all those people around us that we hurt over the years being selfish, self-centered and filled with self-pity when we don't get our way maybe you can identify? I know that pretty much sums up my entire life and was a big gateway into my alcoholism and addiction. Let me give you an example we were asked to give a quick 2 to 3 minute who are we talk. So I let it fly that I had a company that helps people and my plan was to take it worldwide and help millions of people blah blah bla and I felt like I had killed it then I got the following response you are an egotistical arrogant used car salesman at best I would buy into your vision if you were the last man on earth was basically the just of it. I stood there shell shocked in disbelief. When I realized they were right and so I made a conscious decision to listen to how I could change that and it would take months but by the end of the program I no longer sounded like that am happy to report. The next big thing that changed was my accountability we were asked to create personal growth plans basically lists of the things we wanted to accomplish and the people we wanted to be in our lives but in a new way a way that was serving them not using them. Now I had a 2 page list going on complete with dates to be completed by. The great thing about this time though was that I had a team behind me and was actually able to reach out to my team and ask for support in a way that I had never been able to do before and let's be honest you can accomplish so much more with a great coach and amazing team behind you right? Slowly but surely I was able to tell people what they meant to me and I was accomplishing things I had wanted to accomplish for years in a matter of weeks again more freedom. We also would tell people what we really wanted now I don't know about you but I don't like to promise things to people unless I'm sure I can accomplish them I do not like to just say what I really want in my life, my relationships and my career because the truth is at my core I have no idea how to accomplish them and I don't want to look stupid or like an idiot in the process. Instead this process opened me up to be more vulnerable than I have ever been and guess what? Things started to happen and I began to grow not only personally but also spiritually and financially as well. Now not everything happened the way I wanted it to lets be real life never goes the way we think it will right? But at least when things went sideways I had a team to help process it and figure out a positive way to deal with it and not let it stop me as a failure but more of a learning experience. Another great thing that began to happen was that all of my relationships started to get better because they were all based on integrity not just good intentions which we all know just pave the road to hell anyway. When I say relationships I mean every single person I come into contact with not just family and close friends. So I was really getting some growth and then I was asked to come up with 3 words that describe me and my 3 words after a lot of thinking about it were humble, inspirational and powerful. Now the reason I share this is not because those 3 words changed my life at that exact moment because honestly I had done a lot of those over the years in other personal development courses and seminars but it's what happened next because of that that made my life rocket into the 4 dimension. As stated earlier in this book the relationship between my father had come to a complete halt after 20 years of being toxic I had finally ended it 6 years ago and there had been no texts , talks or any contact of any kind. But that night I had a vision or a dream that my father was sitting by himself drinking himself to death alone and miserable and more important than that God had showed me why. You see before I was born my parents had had another son 2 years before me but he had died on the day he was born on that same day my father had called his father and told him the baby had died and that my dad would come by on his way home that night because he was so upset. When my father went over to his parents' house that night no one answered the door he thought it was weird because they knew he was coming over so he opened the door and went in my grandma wasn't home and my dad saw a light on in my grandpas office so he went down to see if my grandpa was asleep instead he found his dad dead of a gunshot wound he had taken his life so in one day my dad had lost his 1st born son and his father a very traumatic day to say the least. My dad had never gotten any counseling or therapy for these events and so his whole life he had kept these things in him and that had made him a very controlling, selfish egotistical man because he was controlled by fear of losing anything else in his life. That and his alcoholism had finally reached their peak and he had alienated everyone in his life my mom had divorced him I had no contact and even my sister was on a strained relationship with him the woman after my mom kicked him out as well and he was completely alone. So I called him and told him not to talk while I told him the same thing I just told you and then I added however because I know what that feels like I am willing to forgive you and help you get your life back in order and be someone to listen to you empathetically so you get some freedom from this crippling series of events. He was almost in tears and said the following 2 things to me the 1st was son that is so HUMBLE of you and the 2nd is how did you know? I told him it had come to me in a dream and that I knew about living in fear and destroying my life and everyone else's around me because of that and that our family of origin had come full circle and I had finally just received some freedom from that and now I wanted to give it back. The other awesome part was that just the day before I had declared my humility as part of my being and for him to say that was definitely a god thing because for the last 43 years my father and I had never a positive relationship around humility in fact he was always telling me I better get some humility never that I had any so this was huge! He also said son I would love your help thank you so much. I am happy to report now 8 months later we have actually gotten together in person and I have kept my commitment to him with weekly phone calls he has now admitted he is an alcoholic and has not had a drink in 6 months as well as he is attending 12 step meeting for that and his other addictions and he is truly a changed man none of this is possible without god but because of him and the work he allowed me to do on myself my dad is back in my life. That's not even all of it I was also able to do the work I needed to in my personal relationships with women that I had struggled with for decades and now not only am I the man I've always wanted to be for the women in my life but I have been able to support a couple of women that I hurt in my younger days as they are going thru really troubling times in their lives now and that feels amazing. But I don't want to get ahead of the story but my relationships with women had suffered over the years because I only equated sex with love and had been in so much fear about my past and never being enough for the women in my life because of 2 things 1 I dint love myself and 2 I didn't trust myself so how could I love or trust anyone and now I had developed both of those traits not only loving myself but also trusting myself and not letting my past dictate my future I was literally walking on clouds by the time I finished this program and I will be eternally grateful to Brad and Jenna Ballard , Micheal Strasner and Christopher Lee not to mention all of my family In the ascension leadership academy thank you all. Now just as I was getting all this freedom back I got a I did not expect it was Christina saying that Lisa was in the hospital and they were giving her last rights and she wanted me there immediately by the time I had gotten there she was already on life support and un responsive. As I was praying over her Christiana called our other friend in the room and he handed me the phone I didn't know who it was and just grabbed it bunny?!!(That was Christina's nickname for me) I was shocked because we had not talked in months and just hearing her voice stopped me cold yes kitty (my nickname for her) is Lisa going to make it? No sweetheart I said I am so sorry but she is dying but I am here and I brought a picture of us to put In her hand and playing her favorite music holding her hand and praying and crying I felt her body get cold and just like that she was gone but at least I had been there as the last person to hold her and I knew the angels had taken her thank god I was not only there but also sober it was June 21st 2016 and I have it tattooed on the side of my finger to remind me these hands are made for praying. After praying about it I called up the family and offered to do the service and give the eulogy and as much as I wanted to do it. It was also very hard because that meant I would have to be in contact with Christina again I mean it was her best friend and I needed to comfort her and I had to put my personal feelings aside for that month while all the arrangements were made. So I got started I made the memory cards and even wrote a beautiful poem that god had directed me to write and then he had me write a letter to Christina from Lisa which at 1st I thought was weird but as I was writing it I had stopped and put my pen down thinking this is stupid the minute I put the pen down Christina texted me about the funeral and so I picked up the pen and finished it because that was definitely gods will but it was hard. The day of the funeral came and I was so nervous not to give my speech but to see Christina I went and bought white and red roses and set up chairs down in a beautiful spot in mission bay overlooking the water I put a memory card and one rose on each chair and on a beautiful sunny day we said goodbye to our Lisa Christina even had the courage to write her own eulogy and I held her hair back and wiped away the tears as she read it it's so weird how death brings us closer together. Then we all went to a club a friend of ours owned and generously donated to us thanks Tattoo Mike Bremer for your support on that one and then of course we acted like we were the best friends all day which made it even harder to say goodbye. Even after professing my love once again and her rebuffing it once again I knew that we were no longer meant to be but it's always hard at least for me to not at least give it one more shot and looking back I know it was god looking out for me because I had never been able to just walk away from a relationship even when it was killing me on the inside. Two days later I was sitting outside on my prayer chair doing my morning prayer and meditation when a hummingbird came within 2 feet of my face and just stayed there looking at me at 1st I was like what in the world? I don't have any hummingbirds at my house or even in my neighborhood I lived in a very dry desert type environment and then it hit me Lisa? Sure enough as soon as I said her name the bird did a little flight around in the air came back and looked at me again and then took off but for the next 2 weeks that little bird would come and fly around me and say hi every morning during my prayer and meditation and I knew that Lisa would always be in my life in one way or another. The next cool thing that happened was that I won something very cool!! I had heard about a really cool event in Las Vegas called amplify live It was a conference of the top entrepreneurs, authors and transformational coaches in the country coming together and I really wanted to go! But once again the price was out of my reach and then one day God sent me a message in the way of a post on Facebook from a guy named Shannon Graham and he said I want to sponsor someone to go to amplify live please send me a video describing what your committed to with your company, Why it would be beneficial for you to attend amplify and then sing your favorite 80's song. I knew this was a sign so I made a video telling him about Buns n Roses and how I really wanted to help more at risk teens and adults that needed 2nd chances but I was stuck in advancing my idea into a legitimate business and I felt if I could learn the skills they were teaching at amplify it would really help me and then I belted out my favorite 80's song I want to rock by twisted sister and sent it. I didn't hear anything back for about a week and started to accept the fact that maybe I wasn't meant to go when I got a message from Shannon saying he would announce the winner the next day on Facebook I was so excited!! So the next day I was so nervous and couldn't wait for this video to come out and finally it did and he said the magic words and these are the people that I want to be my guests and you guessed it I was one of them I was over the moon. Now here is the really cool thing about this story about 3 years ago I had become friends with Shannon on Facebook and we had talked a little on their because we had a lot of the same mindsets and one day he posted he was staying at a resort by my house so I messaged him and asked if I could talk with him in person for a cup of coffee or something and he said yes. So I went to the la costa resort here in San Diego where he was staying and met him at the time I had 26 dollars to my name because I had just lost another job. We ordered 2 smoothies and he got a banana as well I offered to pay for it since he was kind enough to meet me so I said how much and the lady goes 24 dollars. I was like 24 dollars for 2 smoothies and a banana? So I reached into my pocket and pulled out 24 of my last 26 dollars and paid. We then sat down and for 2 hours we gave each other our stories and what we were up to and I was stoked to be talking to this guy who had such great wisdom and vision and at the end I asked Shannon how much would it cost to work with you on this program of yours and he looked me dead in the eye and said Chris I really think we could do some great work together the price is 10k and I responded 10k that's great let me go home and figure out a few things and I'll get back to you and we gave each other a hug and I left. I got to my car and was just sick not only because I was so short of the money but also because I had basically lied to him about being able to do his program. So 10 minutes later I pulled my car over because it was bothering me so much and I sent the following message Hey Shannon I have to be honest with you I just spent 24 of my last 26 dollars buying those damn smoothies and so I am 9,998 dollars short on your price and there's is no way in hell I'm going to be able to come up with it anytime soon and I don't want to be out of integrity with you because I really respect you sorry if I wasted your time and thanks again for hanging out with me and hit send. About 3 minutes later I got the following message back, "hahaha, Chris this is great thank you for being so honest with me most people just would have never responded back and I'll tell you this I can always work with people that have integrity but not a lot of money but I never work with people who have a lot of money and no integrity so let's stay in touch and see what happens". So now 3 years later because I had been honest with him I was able to enter this contest and win so glad I humbled myself that day so now when I really needed some direction here it came in droves because not only was I going to get to sit down with Shannon but also with the top 200 entrepreneurs in the country god is so good. Of course the story doesn't end there on my way to Vegas I had texted a bunch of friends in Vegas to stay with and everyone had something going on so I had nowhere to stay so while eating some del taco in baker CA I went on one of those hotel sites and found a place called the Orleans motel for 40 bucks it was perfect with my connection to New Orleans I figured it was a god shot so I booked the room. I got to Las Vegas and when I rounded the corner off Las Vegas Blvd I realized why it sounded so familiar because it was one block away from my old pill dealers apartment boy does god have a funny sense of humor! After I registered I walked over to the 7-11 on the corner to get some peanut butter pretzels my snack of choice that week and when I walked into the parking lot it was the most surreal moment of my life it had just been robbed and as I looked around it was like that movie the matrix I saw the homeless people laying on the sidewalk the cops had a couple of guys on the ground and I saw myself years before in my car waiting for my dealer to show up and in the midst of all that chaos I realized that I had been insane in my addiction living like this every day in this ghetto cops always arresting someone while I sat by in my car freaking out I was going to get busted or freaking out someone was going to jack me before I got my pills and then I also realized that now I was there for a reason and the reason was because I had won a contest for my company to help people get out of the chaos and start over again and this peace came over me and I was actually really proud of myself so I got my pretzels went back to my room clean and sober and got ready for my big day. The next morning I got to the hotel early because I was so excited but also really scared I mean these people were making 6 or 7 figures and very successful and I had 100 bucks to my name and still needed to eat and find places to stay for the next 3 days so I called my x wife Paula and for once she picked up the phone thank god and I told her where I was and how I got there she was so happy for me and then I started to cry and she said what's a matter? I said these people are all so successful and I'm scared I'm not going to fit in and she said Fumari you are one of them now don't be scared take that amazing personality of yours in there and go kick some ass!! God has always put the best people in my life to teach me things and love me till I learned to love myself and she got me fired up! If that wasn't enough as I was walking into the conference sweet child of mine from guns n roses came on and I knew that God and Buns n roses were a team and I was right where I was supposed to be. Well the conference went above and beyond my wildest expectations I got to hear phenomenal stories from people like Dr Sean Stevenson, Gary Vaynerchuck, Nicholas Kasmich, Keith Yackey, Pete Vargas and a whole bunch of others it was literally the best 3 days of my life and to top it off I had the most amazing lunch with the man himself Shannon Graham and he really put in perspective my vision and what was possible I can't thank him enough for that opportunity. The topper of the whole trip was playing KISS mini golf you can't just be all business baby you gotta keep that Rock n Roll alive too and that day I felt complete as a human being perfect within my imperfections but know God has made me perfect in his eyes and going forward I was going to be the witness to him I have always been destined to be!

Gratitude or Death

As soon as I got back I received another great honor. I had been tending bar and working at Mia Francesca's at night to keep Buns n Roses up and running and one of my regulars happened to work with the largest upscale Kitchen store in the world and one day I got a call that every cook, baker, chef and kitchen gadget person hopes for Hello Chris this is William Sonoma and we were wondering if you would like to come teach a class at our La Jolla Ca store? Would I? Are you kidding?!! So we came up with a plan and Guns and Roses was playing San Diego in a month from when they called so we decided to do a spinoff and have the Buns n Roses welcomes Guns n Roses cupcake competition! We would hold it on August 21st the day before Guns hit town it was advertised and it sold out so fast we decided to have 2 classes we ended up having only one but it had over 30 kids in it! My favorite part was walking in and seeing Buns n roses next to famous chefs like Ina Garten, Ty Florence I felt like I had arrived. I had my #1 assistant Lil Chris as I called him his name was actually Chris so it wasn't too crazy and we prepared the whole thing 70 cupcakes and over 10 lbs. of cream cheese and buttercream frosting and with our new Guns n Roses' t-shirts we hit William Sonoma full on and what a great event we raised hundreds of dollars for no kid hungry charity and had a blast with the kids the winner was EXTREMELY hard to choose but she had designed a cupcake for her sister and it had all of her sisters favorite things which was a princess theme but it was her story that really touched my heart and because it was my story that had gotten me there that day I crowned her the winner. I couldn't believe that I was actually teaching a cupcake decorating class at such a fine institution it was such an honor I mean a guy who lived in the bushes addicted to drugs and alcohol with no hope was now inspiring kids and adults to believe in themselves and with the power of social media I was able to share it with my family back east and all my friends and the people who had supported me and gotten back on my feet it was one of the best days of my life and even though I was really sad that my friend Lisa wasn't there to see me I know she was watching from heaven. I would actually be asked back 2 more times to do events at William Sonoma and I will never forget those people I met and all the joy kids with cupcakes bring to this world. The next day was even better because I got to actually go see Guns n Roses and I took my friend Rochelle of the Saturday cupcake fame and we had a blast. After 3 hours we had to leave because she had to work in the morning and they hadn't played my favorite song so on the way home she made me put it on in the car and we sang it from start to finish together that meant a lot to me because once again I had surrounded myself with people who loved me and wanted me to have the experiences that had made me who I am today and she definitely is in that category.

As August turned to September I was headed to another life changing event. I had not seen my dad in over 7 years or my family in Oregon for that same amount of time and that had been the 1st time for over 10 years before that so I booked a trip to go catch up with everyone and more importantly say good bye to my Uncle Jim who was very ill with cancer and was on a day to day basis. I also wanted to see all my friends in Portland who I rarely saw and most of them had not seen me sober well let's say in recovery because I had been sober a couple of times in the past but not like the beacon of light I had become at this point. It started off great seeing my dad and the next day actually going to an AA meeting with a friend of mine who I had known for over 20 years and who had over 15 years of sobriety and who had done more cocaine with me than pretty much anyone in my life but who is also like a big brother to me. That night I went to one of our old haunts the Belmont Inn over in southeast Portland and caught up with some of my other friends one actually who I have known since high school and it was great to see and remember where I came from and where I am now. The next day caught me up in Long Beach WA for the Rat Rod festival with my friends Jean and Del I had a blast checking out the all the cool Hot rods and of course going to my favorite bakery in the world Cottage Bakery man I love that place!! The next day I was off to Southern or to see Uncle Jim and his wife melody along with all my cousins and aunts and uncles. I sat with my uncle and we talked about how life is too short and how we had missed a lot of time together but in his heart he said I was always the brother he had wanted since he grew up with 3 sisters and he also was so excited for Buns n Roses he was always trying to find me a place in Roseburg Or where he lived to open up a shop I loved that man with all my heart and that day I will never forget. He held on 6 more months but finally passed in March of 2017 RIP Uncle Jim. His wife Melody was also a big supporter of mine and as I walked to my car that day I asked her to come with me I looked her right in the eye and said thank you so much for all you've done for my uncle all the sleepless nights, trips to the hospital, always keeping up the courage to handle him and his cancer and she just started to cry it is still amazing to me how much an acknowledgement to people can mean she said nobody has told me that in so long and it's so hard to always be on for someone when some days you just want to curl up in a ball and pull the covers up. I said oh I know exactly what you mean that was one of the highlights on my trip. I finished off the day seeing my aunts and uncles, cousins and my grandma who I love to death and who just turned 90 and is still going strong! One of my grandmas favorite sayings when I was a kid was Christopher your full of prunes and pond water! She would always tell me that when I told her a fib. The next day I traveled all the way across Oregon and caught my flight home but once again I was complete with letting the people in my life that I loved know just that and that felt good.

Once home I got really cranking with my Rotary club we did a huge project with the boys and girls club re doing an acre of land with a beautiful new garden. Then I got an acknowledgement from marine Sargent for my work with vets and addiction. I hired my second employee Sergei and we were cranking out some Halloween treats for William Sonoma and we also started working with a company called Skate rising that empowers girls from the ages of 5 to 15 to be better people and they kill it the projects they get these beautiful little girls to do are phenomenal and I'm just glad to be able to sponsor them with treats once a month for their skate competitions. Also around this time God put a beautiful woman in my life and I don't want to hex it but let's just say I am no longer sorry for any of the relationships that didn't work out because she is the most amazing woman I have ever met in my life and she is a dead ringer for my favorite pin up model Jane Mansfield. I have always told my mom that I wanted a real life Jayne Mansfield and when my mom saw a picture of her she said oh Christopher there is your real life Jayne Mansfield! She is so much more than just a knockout she is the brakes to my gas and not only keeps me grounded but also makes me a better man. Around Christmas time Buns n Roses did another event with the boys and girls club where we made 150 cupcakes and let each kid decorate their own cupcake and take it home my friend Kambria even dressed up with me as elves and Santa and we had a blast and believe me you can't help get into the Christmas spirit when your sharing the same vision for giving kids that don't have a lot to smile about the gift of fun and laughter as well as the chaos of 150 kids rushing you all at once to decorate their cupcakes oy vey! The best gift I got that year for Christmas was getting to go to see my sister and my mom back in Virginia. Living out on the west coast and working tin the restaurant business makes it almost impossible to spend the holidays together but I also realized the importance of family in my life so my boss made an exception (I think it was the birthday cake I made her that swayed her decision! Lol) and then the following week on new year's eve my friend Kambria and I rang in the new year and my 3 years of sobriety together I had accomplished it again but this time I had God in my life and I was practicing all of the principles in my life and it felt great!

I have had bad knees for pretty much all of my life so it was no surprise to me when I finally had hit a point where my 12 hour work days had literally rendered me barely able to walk I had walked with an embarrassing limp for years but finally even that would have been welcome instead of the pain that shot thru my legs every day. So I went to my orthopedic surgeon's office and met with a wonderful man named Jim who walked me thru and explained that my knees were shot and it was time to schedule a dual knee replacement! We scheduled it for the end of April 2017 it was only the 1st week in January but that was the next available appointment about 2 weeks later getting out of my bed my left leg gave out and sent me rocketing to the floor in agonizing pain it was a Sunday morning and there was nothing I could do so the next day I called the Dr. and went in. Dr. Jim came in and asked what are doing here? I told him what happened and that I was scheduled for surgery for 3 more months what was I going to do? He said give me a minute and walked out. He came back in 2 minutes later and said you're not going to believe this but a woman just cancelled 5 minutes ago which never happens but can you come in next week and get your surgery done? I said no I do believe it Dr. Jim because God is in control and he does this stuff for me all the time!! So the next week I went in and after a 4 hour surgery I had 2 brand new knees! It was excruciatingly painful and the whole theory of going without pain meds came to a quick halt but everyone knew my history so we came up with a plan that I would have to ask for meds they wouldn't just be given to me and they could only be given to me every 4 hours. Even then for the next 2 weeks I was on a regime of Dillauted IV, oxycodone and morphine and to be honest I wasn't ever high or thinking about taking more than I could get. After I got out of the hospital I went to a great inpatient physical therapy place and learned how to walk again and it was also there that god let me know he still had me under watch. I was in a wheel chair and had been in the hospital for over a week at this point and I was feeling kind of low so I prayed to god to send me something to help. I wheeled myself into the workout room for my morning session and saw a woman I recognized but couldn't place, I was still kind of out of it. I asked her what are you doing here she just looked at me and burst into tears. Her name was Diane and she had just gotten a brain tumor removed a couple days before. She had had no warning just got dizzy one day passed out and woke up in the hospital with half of her head shaved. She was so scared but then she told me Chris I love your shares at the AA meetings you always inspire me and I just asked god to help me and within a minute you rolled into the room and then we both started to cry and hugged each other because we knew we were going to be all right. That night a few of her friends came to the hospital and we had an AA meeting in her room it was a breath of fresh air and other friends from AA were also coming into my room as well as my friends Barrett and Blake from my Rotary club in Del Mar and brought me my favorite chips from New Orleans called Zapps chips and doughnuts too!! Of course my friend Kambria who is a nurse also came by and sat for hours just talking to me and listening to me rant about all the things I was going to do as soon as I got out of that hospital I was already going stir crazy! Just a little over 1 week I was already back home and within 2 weeks I could walk on my own slowly and using a walker but at least I could walk. Within a month I was only using a cane and by week 6 I was walking without any help at all a remarkable recovery I always say when the hand of gods favor is on you things move quickly! But the most amazing part of the story is that within 2 weeks I had gotten off all opiates and was just taking anti- inflammatory pills and non- narcotic pain meds what an accomplishment! I had never in my life been able to take any type of pain pill without relapsing what a witness to my relationship with god and the program of Alcoholics Anonymous. On March 15th I celebrated 47 years on this planet with a trip to sea world and doing my favorite things playing air hockey and skee ball with my friend Kambria and we even ate hamburgers and drank milkshakes it was like being a kid all over again what a blessed life I was living!!But he best was still to come. I had been asked to be a facilitator/mentor to some high school age kids at a camp called the RYLA camp which stands for Rotary Youth Leadership Awards camp over 500 kids apply and only about 275 were picked to attend. I had never done anything like this before but I was excited to help in any way I could. Since I had never even made it past my sophomore year in high school I wasn't sure how I could identify with these kids since they were all Juniors and obviously some of the brightest kids in southern California but when I got there it became apparent real quick because these kids as bright as they were still needed someone to help them see how great they actually are and I was more than ready. I was assigned a family of 8 kids both girls and boys and a dorm of 11 boys as well for the sleeping part of it but 11 boys 17 years old doesn't equate to a whole lot of sleep! The 1st day we talked about the issues these kids faced from bullying, gender identifying, addiction and other topics and that was when I knew god had put me there to provide these kids a safe place to process these challenges talk about them and then become empowered to face them and move forward. I shared some of my story not going into detail but the fact that I had left home at 15 and gotten into gangs , drugs and homelessness at their age and I had always wondered why god had done that to me because I wasn't a bad kid I had just made a couple of bad decisions but on that day I told them now I knew why because if I hadn't gone thru all that I would have the empathy and compassion to help them get thru their challenges and that I was going to love the heck out of them all weekend we were a family after all. Their faces just lit up and I knew my purpose for not only being there but going forward in life. By the 3rd day at our final family meeting we did an exercise where we all sat in a circle with our backs facing each other and 2 at a time the kids were chosen to answer 3 questions apiece relating to their lives and their experience at camp and they were to touch the person in the group who they identified with the most on the question. The questions were things like who had the biggest impact on your time at camp? Who do you trust the most in the group? who will you miss the most?, who changed the way you view the world now? And on every question those kids touched me I was blown away and halfway thru I started to weep I couldn't help it. It was like being redeemed not only for all the pain I had gone thru as a kid but also for all the mistakes I had made as an adult. God had worked thru me to change these kids' lives and to let me know that his plan for me was and is going to be a lot more amazing than I had imagined possible. Just another witness to my favorite saying God will not save you from drowning in the ocean to let you drown in your own bathtub. As I finish this book I am starting school again to get my psychology degree, I am attending a speaker conference with some of the top speakers in the country in the next month, I have the most amazing relationships and tribe of people surrounding me and I even have the best relationship with my father that I have ever had. No matter what you are going thru or have gone thru, never give up god always has a plan and just know it isn't the one you have planned because if that was the case you wouldn't receive half the gifts he has in store. So pick yourself up dust yourself off and never leave before the miracle! Not bad for a guy who crawled out of the bushes off Hollywood Blvd a few years ago huh? God Bless you all

- Chris Stewart

Thank You

God , My mom(for always believing in me) My sister Joan (my hero) Michal Simek(best brother ever), Father Michael Nee, Jim Contopulos(Jimdad!), Shannon Graham(mentor & friend), Micheal Zack(worlds best barber),Devin Luther, Amy Dalton, Jenna & Brad Ballard and my ALA family, Peter & Davinna, Doug & Susanna Winter, Chris Gunst,Connie,Vicki, Corey & Belinda Goldstein, Nancy Ross , Chris Williams & the landmark crew, Wendy & Del Murry, Ty & Gwendolyn Shrader, My Portland family Heidi, Robert, Quinn, Mike & Guytona, Cavey, Les,Steve Soto, Tchad ,Lil D, Steve Stewart(love you pop), madball, Lana, Angela,Jennifer Marie, Shelley & Brian,Fast Ross & all my Hollywood family. The Cuneo's , Stewarts, Silvers, Prewitts, Sanfords, Mickelsons, Sierra Colt & Bearcat Tattoo, Theo Mindell & Spider Murphy Tattoo, Lucky ,Lee Bone , Jules and my SF Family, Matt Fuller, Jacob , Rancid, Social Distortion, Volbeat, Kiss, AC/DC, Dee Snider & TMFS, Nikki Sixx , Bullet for my Valetine, Exodus, Dropkick Murphys, Jesse Malin, Jerry A & Tom Pig(RIP), Slayer Hippy, Jackals(PDX) Steve Cosmono(RIP), Slayer, Adam Cardone & Guy(Toilet Boys), Jamie & Hatebreed, Killswitch Engage, Kid Rock, Kix, Sebastian Bach, Stevie Ray Vaughn(RIP), Aerosmith, Jessica (Rabbit)Talin, Dori & Deena Bollen, Rotary 5340, Barrett Smith, Larry & Katie Cook, Carol Eliel(Sunset) Missy Stranser, Danny & Cherri , Blair Robb(Photography) Scott & Dana Mia Francessca , Woody & Patrice, Dan Stuart, My Davanti Family Paolo, Caroline, Perez, Jorge,Edwin , Victor , Mundo & everyone who covered my shifts so I could live this story over the years.Pete Vargas, Nicholis Kusmich. Gary Vaynerchuck, Dr Sean Stephenson , Zig Ziglar, Brendan Burchard, Iyanla Van Zant, Joel Osteen, TD Jakes, Eric Matthews, The Alexanders, Blythe Stein, Rich, Brian, Rob, Aaron, Jeff , Suellen,Dave , Scott, Kate,Nate, Vince, Magda and my chophouse family. Alee Maisam, Lise Cartwright(You are my publishing angel!)Andrew Gill & the 6ft underground guys,Ms Kambria (without you this would have never gotten finished!) To my best friend and biggest cheerleader PLU(There will never be another heart so close to mine Thank you)To everyone I forgot I apologize and will include you in book #2

Copyright ©2018 Chris Stewart all rights reserved

Made in the USA
Columbia, SC
25 August 2018